The
Golden
Girl

The Golden Girl

ROHAN CLARKE

Foreword by Alan Jones

RANDOM HOUSE AUSTRALIA

Random House Australia Pty Ltd
20 Alfred Street, Milsons Point, NSW 2061
www.randomhouse.com.au

Sydney   New York   Toronto
London   Auckland   Johannesburg

First published by Random House Australia 2006

National Library of Australia
Cataloguing-in-Publication Entry

      Clarke, Rohan.
      The golden girl.

      Includes index.
      ISBN 978 1 74166 571 0.
      ISBN 1 74166 571 X.

      1. Cuthbert, Betty, 1938–. 2. Women track and field
      athletes – Australia – Biography. I. Title.

      796.092

Cover photograph Sport the Library
Back cover photograph Frances Andrijich
Back flap photograph Australian Consolidated Press
Portrait of Betty 'pulling down a miracle' opposite title Mandurah Coastal Times

Cover design by i2i Design
Internal design by i2i Design
Printed and bound by Sing Cheong Printing Co. Ltd, Hong Kong

10 9 8 7 6 5 4 3 2 1

contents

contributors

THE AGE, MELBOURNE. We have included an excerpt from *The Age* newspaper of 27 November 1956, as it provides an on-the-spot record of Betty winning the women's 100 metres final.

MIKE AGOSTINI won the 100 yards final at the 1954 British Empire Games in Vancouver, becoming Trinidad and Tobago's first athletics gold medallist. He was designated the world's fastest human in March 1956 by *The New York Times* newspaper. At the Melbourne Olympic Games, Agostini made the final of the 100 metres and 200 metres, finishing sixth and fourth, respectively. He returned to compete in Melbourne in early 1959, before migrating to Australia in September, taking out Australian citizenship shortly afterwards. He has been the consul-general for Trinidad and Tobago in Australia for about 25 years.

JUDY AMOORE was a bronze medallist in the women's 400 metres at the 1964 Tokyo Olympics. She grew up near Melbourne in Mount Macedon and Frankston. Throughout an international career spanning 1964–1976, her only coach was Henri Schubert. In that period, Judy set world records over 400 metres, 440 yards, 800 metres and 880 yards, and her training partners included Pam Kilborn and Charlene Rendina. These days, she calls herself Judy Pollock, following her marriage to Euan Pollock after the Tokyo games. She is a retired primary school teacher who has one son, two daughters and six grandchildren.

RAELENE BOYLE was the world's fastest drug-free sprinter in the early 1970s. She competed at three Olympic Games (1968, 1972 and 1976), winning three silver medals. Like Betty, she made the transition to running 400 metres after a successful career over 100 and 200 metres.

TONY CHARLTON was at the forefront of radio and television broadcasting in Australia for almost 45 years. He covered five Olympic Games, and called the final of the women's 400 metres at the 1964 Tokyo Olympics when Betty Cuthbert claimed her fourth gold medal.

RON CLARKE was one of the world's leading middle- and long-distance runners in the 1960s. He went to two Olympics, winning a bronze medal in the men's 10,000 metres in Tokyo in 1964. He is just as well known for lighting the Olympic Flame during the opening ceremony of the 1956 Melbourne Olympics. He is currently Mayor of the Gold Coast, Queensland.

GLORIA COOKE competed at the 1956 Melbourne Olympics, 1958 Commonwealth Games and the 1960 Rome Olympics. At the 1956 Olympics, she finished sixth in the final of the 80 metres hurdles won by Shirley Strickland. Gloria was a team-mate of Betty at the Western Suburbs Women's Athletics Club, before Betty left to join Cumberland after the Melbourne Olympics. Gloria's coach was Bill Harrison. She now lives in Frenchs Forest and is a close friend of Marlene Mathews.

NORMA CROKER ran fourth in the 200 metres at the 1956 Melbourne Olympics. She teamed with Shirley Strickland, Fleur Mellor and Betty Cuthbert to win gold in the 4x100 metres relay. She also competed at the 1960 Rome Olympic Games. She is now known as Norma Fleming, having married Lloyd Fleming shortly after the Melbourne Olympics.

HERB ELLIOTT is one of the world's greatest middle-distance runners. He won the men's 1500 metres at the 1960 Rome Olympics and broke the four-minute mile barrier on 17 occasions. In 42 races from 1957 to 1961, he was never beaten over 1500 metres or a mile.

DAWN FRASER has the rare distinction of attending three successive Olympics, winning gold medals in the women's 100 metres freestyle in Melbourne, Rome and Tokyo.

IAN HEADS, prolific sports writer and commentator, was 13 when Betty first won gold. He shares his vivid recollections.

MARJORIE JACKSON won the women's 100 and 200 metres at the 1952 Helsinki Olympics. She finished her career with seven gold medals from the Commonwealth Games and 10 world records. In late 2001, she was appointed Governor of South Australia.

PAUL JENES, President of the Association of Track and Field Statisticians (AFTS) and Official Statistician for Athletics Australia, provides the impressive hard facts and figures that help to demonstrate part of Betty's allure. He is also responsible for the statistics section at the back of the book.

BRUCE MCAVANEY is one of Australia's leading sporting broadcasters. He has been to every Olympic Games since 1984.

MARLENE MATHEWS was Betty Cuthbert's great rival. She won bronze medals in the women's 100 metres and 200 metres at the 1956 Melbourne Olympic Games, but was a controversial omission from the team that won the 4x100 metres relay. Marlene later won gold medals in the 100 yards and 220 yards at the 1958 Commonwealth Games in Cardiff. She set a world record for the 440 yards in an interclub race at the Sydney Sports Ground on 6 January 1957. The following year, she set two world records there-the 100 yards and 220 yards-in the space of 48 hours during the national championships.

ANN PACKER represented Great Britain at the 1964 Tokyo Olympics. She finished second behind Betty in the women's 400 metres, then won the gold medal in the 800 metres. (Her quote is sourced from *The Pursuit of Sporting Excellence by David Hemery*.)

(JULIUS) JUDY PATCHING is said to be Betty's closest friend in athletics. Their relationship evolved after he was the starter in each of Betty's three gold medal winning races in Melbourne. He affectionately called her Skipper after Betty was made captain of the women's athletic team. Judy went to 12 Olympic and three Commonwealth Games. His roles have included chief starter at the 1956 Melbourne Olympic Games, section manager of athletics in 1960, assistant general manager in 1964 and *chef de mission* for the Australian team in 1968 and 1972. He was also secretary-general of the Australian Olympic Committee (AOC) and founding secretary-general for the Oceania Zone of the International Olympic Committee (IOC).

DAVID PRINCE won a silver medal in the 120 yards hurdles at the 1962 Perth Commonwealth Games. He won eight individual Australian titles in the 120 yards and 220 yards hurdles from 1961 to 1964. He captained the Australian track and field team to the 1966 Jamaica Commonwealth Games. Later, he was president of Athletics Australia from 1989 to 1997.

JIM WEBSTER is a lifelong friend of Betty's. In 1966, he helped her write her original autobiography, *Golden Girl*.

foreword

The Golden Girl indeed!

Betty Cuthbert entered our lives in an unforgettable way.

For those born much later than 1956, it may be difficult to comprehend how remarkable are the achievements of Betty Cuthbert and how appalling is our teaching of history that there are some who don't understand the indelible place she holds in the hearts of millions of Australians.

This magnificent illustrated biography on the 50th anniversary of the 1956 Melbourne Olympic Games will go some way towards repairing that omission.

In 1956, I was just a kid in the bush.

Betty Cuthbert was the reason I knew the Olympic Games were on.

But it wasn't until the newspapers of the day heralded her triumphs on Tuesday, 27 November 1956 that some Australians, and the rest of the world, knew that a young girl from Ermington in Sydney was serving sporting notice on the world of track and field.

It was a big new world for all of us.

Harry Gordon, in his wonderful book, *Australia and the Olympic Games*, set the scene for the remarkable triumphs which were to follow when he wrote, 'When the Olympic Games moved into Melbourne from 22 November to 8 December 1956, it was as if the city had been brushed by a certain magic. Nothing before or since—no football final, or Test Cricket Match, or Melbourne Cup, neither the departure of Burke and Wills nor the arrival of the Beatles—has ever evoked such sheer emotional involvement from the whole community …'

Well, into all of that—a veritable vortex of emotion, apprehension and heightened expectation—stepped an innocent, unassuming and (some thought) hopelessly unprepared young girl from the suburbs of Sydney. Paradoxically, not far from where the 2000 Olympics were held.

She was a twin, Betty Cuthbert.

And that Golden Girl, with straw-coloured hair and a distinctive, wide-mouthed manner that made her look as if she was roaring excitedly down the track, took the 1956 Olympic Games by storm.

And with it, the nation and the world of track and field.

It was as if her life had been driven towards this explosive climax that lasted through the Melbourne Olympics. There, in 1956, and later on in Rome in 1960, Betty Cuthbert became the emblem of Australian achievement.

She had been overshadowed in 1956 before the Olympic Games trials, and even after the Olympic Games were over. She went into the Melbourne Games without ever having won a senior State Championship. But in nine glorious days that ended on 1 December 1956, she won three gold medals—the 100 metres, 200 metres, and 4x100 metres relay—emulating the legendary Fanny Blankers-Koen and writing herself forever into the hearts and history of Australians.

She was to repeat it again in 1964, but in an altogether different way.

It was the first time, ever, a women's 400 metres had been run at the Olympic Games. And it came after the unsuccessful defence of her Olympic titles in Rome, when Betty had suffered a hamstring injury along the way. Triumph, in Rome, went to an unbelievable black American, Wilma Rudolph, who etched her name into Olympic immortality in the same way as Betty had four years previously.

Betty Cuthbert had lived on a four-acre flower farm at Ermington near Parramatta. She was the Ermington Primary School champion over 50 and 75 yards. Wilma Rudolph had learnt to run by racing her 17 brothers and sisters to the dinner table. They deserve being mentioned in the same context.

After Rome, for Betty, it was time to retire.

And she did.

But it wasn't long before the comeback was in place in 1962.

Who will ever forget it?

Betty's individual failure at the Perth Commonwealth Games was almost impossible to endure. The press and the public were unsympathetic. It was said she was wasting her time. It was even reported that she was to be withdrawn from the relay team.

But Betty Cuthbert didn't want to let the girls down. And so was born one of the most dramatic moments in Australia's track and field history.

I remember well listening to the call on the ABC.

Australia were no chance in the relay. Brenda Cox, the young schoolgirl from Brisbane, ran the third leg and handed the baton to Betty Cuthbert, 5 metres behind Betty Moore of England. The commentator's voice bore the inflection of inevitable defeat.

And then something snapped inside the great Cuthbert. And, in one of the brilliant pieces of commentary, something also overtook the commentator. In dramatic tones, he described how the Melbourne Olympics, in one short 100 metres relay leg, was being revisited.

Cuthbert swallowed up the Perth stadium. The gap narrowed from 5 metres to 4 to 3. Twenty metres out, Betty Cuthbert was still a metre behind. At 10 metres, she was level. And with a last desperate kick, she went past Betty Moore to secure gold for Australia.

The Golden Girl was back.

Betty and her coach, June Ferguson, knew that her chances of further Olympic gold lay in the inaugural Olympic 400 metres in the Tokyo Olympics of 1964.

By March 1963, it was the Cuthbert of old, smashing world records for the 400 metres and 440 yards in the one race.

Then she broke the 440 yards record again, running 53.3 seconds.

Think of it.

That's 42 years ago.

Well, by the time Tokyo came around, Betty Cuthbert wasn't even the favourite for the gold medal, let alone the world record holder. That belonged to a North Korean girl. But she wasn't competing.

The favourite was Britain's Ann Packer.

Packer and Cuthbert made the final, along with another Australian, Judy Amoore. And what a final it was!

It was the first time in Olympic history that a women's 400 metres had been run.

Anything could happen.

Cuthbert in lane two; Packer in lane six. Betty had the look on them all the way. Going into the final bend, Betty Cuthbert had passed Judy Amoore and there was only Packer to beat. As they straightened, Packer was only a fraction behind Cuthbert and there was a hell of a head wind. But Betty, to the cheers of every Australian at home, was fighting with everything she could muster for a remarkable place in Olympic history.

The very best race callers would have called it Packer and Cuthbert, Cuthbert and Packer.

But Betty Cuthbert was never one to buckle.

She won, not comfortably, but decisively, in 52 seconds. A tenth of a second outside the North Korean's world record.

Many years later, Betty described her victory in this way: 'It wasn't really me running … it was as if my body had been taken over. And I felt at great peace afterwards. I asked God, "Have I done enough?"'

She had done enough, all right.

She had won her fourth Olympic gold medal and joined the immortals of track and field.

The story is all here, in this glorious volume.

These are just some of the highlights.

I have said before, publicly, that in the happiness stakes, we owe Betty Cuthbert heaps.

Betty, you have made us so happy, we don't just want to cry, we want to recall over and over again your golden moments.

And thankfully, we can do that here with *The Golden Girl*.

ALAN JONES AO
Broadcaster, Radio 2GB 873; TCN Channel 9 Today Show
Sydney 2006

preface

One might well ask why Betty Cuthbert is so revered, so honoured and so idolised, not only by her contemporaries, but also by millions who never saw her run.

There are a whole host of factors. For a start, she was an incredible champion: she won four Olympic gold medals over an eight-year period and has been the holder of almost every women's world track record from 60 metres to 440 yards.

But there's much, much more to the Golden Girl phenomenon than that.

Betty was always so very humble in victory; so kind in defeat. She was the girl with the straw-coloured hair and loving smile, and that unmistakable wide-mouthed expression when she ran. She came out of Sydney's working-class west. She never personally whipped up any headline-grabbing controversy, despite being blighted by acts of natural disaster and unkindness. Years after her running career was over, she was stricken with multiple sclerosis. But through it all, she has remained our lovable, unaffected, untainted Betty.

Half a century after the world was introduced to the Golden Girl, everyone continues to adore her. This book is a heart-felt celebration of Betty's life: her achievements on and off the field, her integrity, her compassion and her warmth.

JIM WEBSTER
Sydney 2006

This book celebrates the golden anniversary of Australia's original Golden Girl winning gold. During the course of her remarkable yet unassuming life journey since that exhilarating moment in 1956, Betty Cuthbert has touched the hearts, spirits and imaginations of countless Australians. We have spoken with many of those who know and love her personally; who have competed with and against her; travelled with her to represent Australia in Commonwealth and Olympic Games. In this book, we delight in sharing some of their memories and recollections of Betty, weaving together a tribute that showcases Betty's life, her achievements on and off the field and—above all—her extraordinary spirit: her capacity to meet every challenge with strength, good humour and faith.

ROHAN CLARKE
Sydney 2006

'*It was a hell of a thrill to be able to train with*

Very special and very fast

one of the best sprinters in the world.'

etty Cuthbert was born in the Sydney suburb of Merrylands on 20 April 1938, during the Great Depression. Her twin sister Marie, nicknamed 'Midge', arrived 20 minutes later—a shock to all concerned, including their mother. Les and Marion Cuthbert already had a daughter, Jean, aged six, and a son, John, aged four.

When the children were still young, their father opened a small nursery at Ermington, near Parramatta in Sydney's west, where Betty lived into her adult years. It fronted a busy road which meant, later, that it was an easily-found location for tourists and sports nuts wanting to see where the Golden Girl lived and perhaps catch a glimpse.

Betty's upbringing, schooling and way of life were simple: the Cuthberts were not rich. But it was a close, loving family and one that gave her wonderful support throughout her sporting life and everything that followed. Her mother became a timekeeper in athletics for Betty's sake, and came to love the sport so much that she continued timekeeping well after Betty had finished racing.

Athletics had been severely affected during World War II, but by the time Betty was in primary school, club and championship competition had resumed in Australia. The sport was segregated in those days: men and women had their own organisations and competed separately. Athletics meetings were held on grass tracks, usually football and cricket ovals, and the amateur code was strictly enforced by rigid officialdom.

There was no sponsorship and little if any government funding for sport. As Marlene Mathews explains, 'We didn't get everything given to us. We didn't even have spikes given to us. We had to pay for everything. At state and club level, we had to pay for our uniforms. And we had to raise money to go overseas for Commonwealth and Olympic Games. I think we were given an allowance of two and sixpence [25 cents] a day when we went away to compete. We could accept a trophy to the value of about 15 pounds [30 dollars]. No money'.

Betty's unmistakable, toothy smile was evident in many of her childhood photographs.

top left: *John, Jean, Midge and Betty (front left) pose for a family snap.*

top right: *Betty (centre) with playmates.*

bottom: *With their golden locks and radiant smiles, it is difficult to tell Betty and Midge apart. Betty is on the left.*

previous spread: *Baby Betty (right) with her twin sister, Marie, nicknamed Midge.*

left: *Two peas in a pod: Betty and Midge, who is slightly taller, were inseparable for much of their childhood.*

opposite top left: *Betty and Midge have a little fun at a photographer's expense.*

centre: *Betty (back row, far right) seems comfortable whenever she is wearing her sports gear.*

top right: *Betty poses in her school uniform.*

bottom: *Betty's athletic prowess coincided with a growth spurt and she was one of the tallest girls in her year at Parramatta Home Science High School. In this photo, Betty is standing in the second row, fifth from the left.*

PARRAMATTA
HOME SCIENCE
HIGH SCHOOL
3AH's 1953

International competition for Australians was limited to the Olympic and Commonwealth Games (Empire Games, as they were known then) and an occasional Trans-Tasman competition against New Zealand. It was rare for athletes to compete overseas and female athletes had to have chaperones.

Betty was eight when she ran her first proper foot race. The occasion was sports day at Ermington Primary School: Betty wore a long, drab tunic and ran in bare feet. Quick and lean as a whippet, she won the 50 yards and 75 yards races easily, keeping up the new family tradition her sister Jean and brother John had established. (Oddly enough, neither of their parents showed any aptitude for sport.)

Betty kept on winning races—in fact, she wasn't beaten again for three years—and when she progressed to Parramatta Home Science School she met the woman who was to help change her life. Their first encounter was formal: Mrs June Ferguson was the school's physical education teacher.

As June Maston, she had been a distinguished runner herself: one of only nine women in Australia's team at the 1948 London Olympics where, although she did not qualify in the long jump, she won a silver medal in the 4x100 metres relay. That year, the Dutch relay team—which included the legendary Fanny Blankers-Koen—took home the gold. (June later married Jack Ferguson, a water polo player from the same Games.)

It didn't take long for June to be impressed by Betty's barefoot wins at school races and she invited Betty to join Western Suburbs Athletics Club, where she was the women's coach. Thus began the coach–athlete relationship and close friendship that endured until June's passing many years later. In fact, June was the only formal coach Betty ever had. And while they had differences of opinion, even the occasional argument, June's strategies and Betty's willingness to learn turned out to be a dynamic combination.

Tony Charlton recalls: 'Betty freely admits she knew nothing about the art of sprinting when she joined forces with June Ferguson'. And David Prince sheds light on June's approach, commenting that she 'was a very strict disciplinarian, a good planner and … a very good communicator'.

Sign of the times: as was customary in the 1950s, girls running in school athletics carnivals wore a belted sports dress—quite often with a shirt and tie. BETTY CUTHBERT PERSONAL COLLECTION

When Betty was 13 years old, she won a place in the New South Wales schools' team competing at the inaugural Australian Schools Championships in Hobart, Tasmania, where she won the under 14 100 yards and came second in the 75 yards. (Girls running in school meets in those days wore a belted sports dress which came to just above the knee. They also wore a shirt and quite often a tie, depending on the school.)

To June Ferguson, Betty's untapped natural ability was obvious. She saw her winning potential, and encouraged and coached her to refine that unconventional style with its ungainly, uncoordinated stride and high knee lift. Says contemporary, Marlene Mathews: 'Betty ran over the ground with a longer stride. She didn't have the leg drive like me. We always said Betty ran over the ground whereas I used the ground to my advantage.

'Our running action was a lot different to what you see with today's athletes, which has adjusted to the synthetic tracks. There's a lot more resilience in the synthetic tracks than we ever had on a grass or cinders track.'

Even then, Betty ran with her mouth wide open and gulping air. June, realising this quirk did not affect Betty's speed or performance, chose not to alter what was to become one of the Golden Girl's trademarks.

Betty was still 13 when she started training seriously several nights a week and began competing in interclub athletics. It was 1951. Many of her peers were older than she was. Gloria Cooke was amongst them, and recalls those early days: 'I was living at Earlwood and had just turned 15 when I started athletics in the summer of 1948–49 … A friend took me along to Western Suburbs Women's Athletics Club and that is where I met Betty and Marlene. Bet was only very young—she's three-and-a-half years younger than me. My Mum, Una, who became secretary of the club, was very close to her. Mum used to boost her up and look after her'.

June taught Betty to warm up properly by jogging and stretching before training or a race. She introduced her to spiked running shoes and to starting blocks, and taught her how to use the blocks to get away quickly. From a very early stage in their partnership, they set their sights on the Melbourne Olympics. By age 17,

Betty was introduced to grass tracks from an early age, and developed a unique style of sprinting. THE HERALD & WEEKLY TIMES PHOTOGRAPHIC COLLECTION

Betty was competing in senior events although she was still a junior. And she was fortunate in having strong competition in Sydney.

She often raced against Fleur Mellor, who was two years her senior and had lots of ability, as well as having the same coach (Jim Monaghan) as the famous 'Lithgow Flash', Marjorie Jackson. The pair had some terrific sprint battles and when Betty— who by now had grown to a height of 169 centimetres with long legs—gained ascendancy over Fleur, their names were linked as prospective champions and possible members of the Australian team at the forthcoming 1956 Melbourne Olympics.

Marlene Mathews was Betty's major competitor during the mid 1950s. Although they were training patners, Marlene vividly remembers their friendly rivalry: 'I grew up in Strathfield and ran for Western Suburbs, which was the same club as Betty, until June Ferguson left and formed her own club, Cumberland, at North Epping Oval.

'In the mid to late 1950s, Bet and I were probably the two top women sprinters in the world. We ran against each other every Saturday at interclub meets. We were fortunate to have that competition and I believe that's what brought the best out [in] us. So it was of great benefit. There was never a case of "I don't want to run against her today in case she beats me". We didn't avoid competition.

'We were always gracious in defeat. When Betty and I were running, it was either one of us that won. We never showed any disrespect or jealousy. It never entered our minds. If someone was better than you on a particular day, you accepted it and were happy for her. So there was never any animosity even though there was a lot of rivalry.

'Bet and I were never close friends. We were rivals on the track and friends off the track. But we never mixed socially unless it was at official functions. We saw a bit more of each other in the early days after we both retired.'

It is true that Betty would not allow herself to be distracted by boys and socialising during this period. Her focus was on athletics and she made an active decision not to get mixed up with the opposite sex. She was 19 when she had her first date.

But when it came to training, segregation was not an issue and Betty made a good friend and running mate in David Prince. David has fond memories of meeting Junc and Betty, and training against the girl who went on to win gold: 'In 1954, prior to the Melbourne Olympic Games, I was a youngster succeeding in school athletics in Sydney. A group had established Ryde-Hornsby Athletic Club at Epping Oval. It became the hub for men's athletics in that particular area of the northern suburbs and attracted quite a few people to come and train on Monday, Wednesday and Sunday mornings.

'It was at that time that I met June Ferguson, who had competed at the 1948 Olympic Games. June had begun teaching a group of young women sprinters, including Betty Cuthbert. The women would occasionally train with our club at Epping Oval. Eventually, the ladies formed the Cumberland Women's Athletic Club.

'As a youngster, I trained on and off with Betty even though I had another coach. My running times in 1956 over the 100 and 200 were just a metre or two faster than Betty's. So it was a good environment for her to be running against me in an event where she could stretch out a little bit more, rather than running with the girls, where she was much faster. We became friends through that.

'Betty was able to beat me on some occasions, for example, when we were practising our starts, doing 30 and 40 metre dashes. It didn't particularly bother me. I was only a pup. I turned 15 in 1956, whereas Betty was 18 when she went to Melbourne for the Olympics. But I still thought, "Pull your finger out, don't let this happen again". You knew you were racing against someone who was very special and very fast.

'It was tremendously inspirational to run with Betty. I would go to training with the knowledge there wasn't ever going to be an easy session. She trained very hard. Even though I could just beat her in 1956, it was a hell of a thrill to be able to train with one of the best sprinters in the world—and know you were doing something to help her, but at the same time help yourself.'

Meanwhile, Betty had finished school and, after a few months in a factory making baby clothes, decided that she didn't like being cooped up indoors and went to work for her father in the nursery. As a propagator, she took slips from shrubs and trees and sowed them into sand boxes. When she wasn't busy doing that, she was selling stock to customers, making out invoices, assembling orders and generally making herself useful. She relished the quiet life the nursery provided, as it allowed her to focus on her training. Any spare time she had went into breeding and selling budgerigars and caring for her goldfish. Of that period in her life, Betty says: 'I liked the nursery and Dad knew I liked it. My sister Marie was the inside girl and did all the housework. She did my share of the housework because I [was too busy working and training and] couldn't. She was always supportive and she has never been jealous. She has just been there for me'.

David Prince recalls: 'Betty's work ethic was extraordinary. She worked all day and every day outdoors—and then came to training. Occasionally, she would say, "I'm so tired. I've been on my feet all day in Dad's nursery". Yet she would still do a two-hour training session'.

Amateur status was paramount. As Marlene Mathews explains, 'Most of us had to work. In those days, we were lucky that we had jobs. Just before the Olympics, I lost my job as an office assistant with the New Zealand trade commissioner because I flew to Melbourne to have treatment for a hamstring injury with George Saunders.

'We had to go to school or we had to go to work. The night I broke the world record for 100 yards, I had been to work until lunchtime at Behr-Manning where I was a secretary.

'It didn't do us any harm. I don't believe that you can eat, sleep and spend your whole life living your sport. I think you've got to have other interests. But what we did in training probably wouldn't even constitute a warm-up today.'

By the end of 1955, Betty's 100 yards time of 11.0 seconds and 100 metres time of 11.9 seconds ranked her 17th in the world. In early 1956, she ran within inches of Marlene Mathews over 220 yards. They both recorded times of 24.0 seconds—which equalled Marjorie Jackson's world record set in Vancouver in 1954.

The 1956 Australian Championships for women were held in March on a very sodden, muddy Brisbane Cricket Ground. In her heat of the 100 yards, Betty finished a disappointing third behind Shirley Strickland and Wendy Hayes in 11.0 seconds and was eliminated. But by the time she ran the 220 yards, she was in top form. Not only did she achieve her first competition win over Marlene Mathews; she also won the title in 25.0 seconds.

Betty's career as a runner was now well under way. She was selected in a squad of 24 women to train for the 1956 Olympics. From June onwards, in the lead-up to the October trials, there were special Sunday competitions. On 16 September, Betty won the 100 metres in 11.8 seconds and then ran an astounding 23.2 seconds in the 200 metres, breaking Marjorie Jackson's world record by two tenths of a second and improving her own personal best by 0.7 seconds. Two weeks later she ran 24.0 seconds over 220 yards to equal the old imperial record.

The Olympic trials were held at Royal Park in Melbourne and Betty won the sprint double in 11.7 and 23.7 seconds, beating Marlene Mathews and Norma Croker to gain selection. It was now clear that Betty Cuthbert would not be needing the Games tickets she had purchased earlier in the year. She gave them to her brother.

top: *Ankle-deep in mud: the national championships at the Gabba in 1956 were marred by extraordinarily poor weather. Shirley Strickland leads Betty Cuthbert.* BETTY CUTHBERT PERSONAL COLLECTION

below: *Athletics gave Betty the opportunity to travel interstate and abroad, which was a privilege for Australians in the 1950s and 1960s. Here, Betty and New South Wales team-mates board a plane. Marlene Mathews, Betty, Maureen Wright and Gloria Cooke.* THE HERALD & WEEKLY TIMES PHOTOGRAPHIC COLLECTION

opposite: *Even before the Games, Betty's ability was beginning to attract attention. Reproduced here is a press clipping from her memorabilia that reflects this interest and speculation.* BETTY CUTHBERT PERSONAL COLLECTION

Asked if Betty would be fit for the 1956 Olympic Games Miss Ferguson replied: 'My word she will.'

MARJORIE JACKSON
World Champion of Today

BETTY CUTHBERT
World Champion of Tomorrow?

Brushed by a certain magic

'It was the most wonderful week in my life.'

When Betty Cuthbert arrived at the Games Village in Melbourne in November 1956, she was just 18 years old. It was the first time she had been away from her family, her friends and her coach, June Ferguson, for any length of time. Suddenly, she found herself living the dream that she and June had dared to imagine, and worked so hard to achieve.

Everywhere she went within the Village, there were world-class athletes representing nations and cultures from around the globe. Betty recognised some from photographs: Vladimir Kuts, Bobby Morrow, Gordon Pirie, Ron Delaney, Charlie Dumas, Parry O'Brien, Alain Mimoun, the Reverend Bob Richards, Milt Campbell, Hal Connolly and Olga Fikotova.

These world-renowned sporting stars were sharing the same training track, eating in the same dining hall and living just a few streets away. For Betty, the shy, naive girl from Ermington, it was extraordinarily exciting, overwhelming and at times, a little daunting.

The excitement was contagious. From every part of Australia, people of all ages were flocking to Melbourne to soak up the atmosphere and experience first-hand the wonder of the Olympic Games.

IAN HEADS Harry Gordon wrote beautifully many years later [in *Australia and the Olympic Games*] of a city 'brushed by a certain magic'. And to a wide-eyed 13-year-old from Sydney, indeed it seemed that way in Melbourne on those late spring days of November 1956. A sports-loving kid, I had been taken out of school (yippee!) and packed aboard an overnight Melbourne-bound inter-city coach by my mum——for reasons that still tantalise, all these years on. My mother was a war widow who took in sewing to raise the few extra shillings to get us all by; miraculously, she had scraped up enough to finance the project of sending her son to the Olympics.

National euphoria ran high. Friendliness and cooperation were themes within the Australian camp, and throughout the Village. Sportsmanship that supported

previous spread: *Betty claims her first gold medal in the 100 metres at the Melbourne Olympics.* AAP/AP PHOTO/GOPA

OLYMPIC GAMES

MELBOURNE

The Coat of Arms of the City of Melbourne

following spread: *An estimated crowd of 103,000 witnessed Ron Clarke carry the Olympic torch around the Melbourne Cricket Ground on Thursday, 22 November 1956.*

friendly rivalry was considered an honourable attribute. The intense and sometimes bitter competitiveness of modern Olympics was almost non-existent, and certainly not a preoccupation for the public. Nor were many of the other issues that have plagued the sporting world in recent times.

MIKE AGOSTINI Drugs have been around in sport forever. There were drugs in the ancient Olympics, mainly natural potions made from herbs and plants. But people like Betty Cuthbert, John Landy and Marjorie Jackson would never have considered taking drugs.

Accepting money was an even bigger issue for athletes, who were considered to be amateurs at that time. It was worse to be found guilty of receiving any kind of financial benefit than being caught taking drugs.

Although coach June Ferguson, nursing her newborn third child, was not present to offer moral and technical support, Betty was surrounded by her team-mates, many of whom were long-term training partners and friends. Shirley Strickland, with maturity and confidence gained in London and Helsinki, actively supported the other young women in the team, and Betty was also lucky enough to be sharing a room with her old rival and good friend, Fleur Mellor. The 400 metres runner Kevan Gosper, who much later became a member of the International Olympic Committee (IOC), took Betty under his wing, too, and treated her like a kid sister, counselling and coaching her between her frequent phone conversations with June. The slight stiffness she had developed in her right leg was not considered a problem, and certainly didn't slow her down.

After almost two months of rain, Melbourne turned on a stunningly sparkling day for the Opening Ceremony on Thursday 22 November, 1956. Betty recalls that she felt 'like a tiny little dot' marching onto the Melbourne Cricket Ground with the other 290 Australian team members, cheered on by more than 103,000 wildly patriotic spectators. And although she attended two more Opening Ceremonies as a competitor, she still says 'Melbourne was the best'.

Four thousand pigeons fluttered into the sky as Prince Philip, Duke of Edinburgh, gave the opening speech. There was a fanfare of trumpets, a 21-gun salute and distance runner, Ron Clarke, ran into the stadium with the Olympic torch, sprinted up the steps and lit the Olympic flame. The Archbishop of Melbourne delivered the Dedicatory Address and a choir sang the Olympic Hymn and Handel's 'Hallelujah Chorus'. On behalf of the 4000 plus sportsmen and women from 67 nations, mile runner John Landy, later to become Governor of Victoria, delivered the Olympic Oath: 'We swear that we will take part in the Olympic Games in loyal competition, respecting the regulations which govern them and desirous of participating in them in the true spirit of sportsmanship for the honour of our country and for the glory of sport'.

And in Royal Newcastle Hospital, Betty's older sister, Jean, gave birth to her first child, Stephen, making Betty Cuthbert an auntie for the first time. Needless to say, this exciting and potentially distracting news was kept from Betty for several days.

Having captured world headlines for breaking the four-minute mile, Victorian John Landy was asked to read the athlete's Olympic Oath during the Opening Ceremony. The speech has been read at every Games since 1956. THE HERALD & WEEKLY TIMES PHOTOGRAPHIC COLLECTION

IAN HEADS Sunny Melbourne in that Games of '56, surely swept away the blues for everyone lucky enough to be there. And so it did for me. I stayed at Hawthorn with relatives—my uncle and aunt, Frank and Hilda Appleton—the pair of them not so long back from post-war work in Europe. I strongly suspect they paid for the sheaf of tickets that were thrust into my hand, opening the door to the thrilling, transient carnival about to unfold at the Melbourne Cricket Ground.

I stayed exactly a week, went only to the MCG (Opening Ceremony and track and field) and gathered memories and impressions that have stayed with me powerfully for these 50 years. I recall that Thursday, November 22 Opening Ceremony, seated alongside my Uncle Frank, as the most wonderful example imaginable of the 'shared experience'. To be there in the midst of a crowd of 103,000 as the world's athletes marched, Ron Clarke ran the torch to a great, rippling roar from the crowd and an early hero, John Landy, took the oath, was overwhelming and unforgettable. The feeling that day was joyous from the moment we stepped from the tram and were swept up in the teeming crowd marching across the pedestrian bridge and into that great and ancient ground with its brick red track.

The Games of the XVI Olympiad had begun.

For the briefest of interludes, the athletes were able to relax and soak up the atmosphere, before the competition began in earnest. And Betty was her normal sweet, unassuming self.

DAVID PRINCE After the Opening Ceremony, as typical young kids, my mate and I wandered out of the MCG. Not knowing what to do next, we walked over to the Punt Road Oval, the old Richmond footy club ground. The whole of the Australian team was assembled over there saying hello to their Mums and Dads. (Today, you wouldn't get in because there would be heavy security.)

I remember Betty—it wasn't me approaching her. She walked over and said, 'Hey Dave, come over and say hello'. At that stage she hadn't won anything. There were no airs or graces. Her attitude wasn't, 'Oh, I don't have to talk to that 15-year-old kid. I'm mixing over here with all the other stars'. She made us feel fantastic as young kids.

opposite: *As a consolation for missing selection in the Australian team, middle-distance runner Ron Clarke was given the honour of lighting the Olympic flame. (He later represented Australia at the 1964 and 1968 Olympics.)* AUSTRALIAN PICTURE LIBRARY

46

IAN HEADS The next day, the serious business began. That first morning at any Olympics is a wonderful time, as I came increasingly to appreciate at future Games I attended (Moscow, Atlanta and Sydney). The tumult and the shouting and the razzamatazz from the Opening Ceremony has faded into colourful memory. At the break of the day the best in the world are suddenly out there, running and rowing and lifting and throwing, and the Games are really on.

The events of Day 1, Melbourne 1956, will stay with me for as long as memory allows. Australians won two medals that day——Alan Lawrence a bronze in the 10,000 metres and Charles 'Chilla' Porter a silver in the high jump. What extraordinary theatre those two contests produced! The courage of Lawrence in winning his medal behind the brutal and brilliant Russian Vladimir Kuts brought tears to my eyes.

The high jump shoot-out between Australia's Porter and the American Charles Dumas remains among the most dramatic things I have ever seen in sport. Trailing deep into the Melbourne dusk it seemed an event without ending, as Porter and Dumas punched and counter-punched for hours. Finally, in deepening gloom, Dumas soared over the bar at 6 foot 11-and-a-quarter inches [211.5 centimetres] on the final jump of the day to take the gold——and I sprinted from the stadium to catch a tram home to Hawthorn before night closed in.

The next day, came Betty Cuthbert …

Even a sporting tenderfoot, whose interest flicked restlessly from cricket to boxing to rugby league to tennis and most stops along the way, knew of Betty well by then. Having been seemingly in the shadow of her friend/rival Marlene Mathews, she had emerged spectacularly in the run-up to the Games with a world record run [in the 200 metres] and then the taking of the sprint double at the Olympic trials. An early interest in the timeline of sport, generated by the excellent magazines of the time, *Sporting Life* and *Sports' Novel*, even then gave me a sense that Betty and Marlene were continuing on the wonderful work of gold medallists Marjorie Jackson and Shirley Strickland at the 1952 Helsinki

Olympics and perhaps others before. I had already 'met' the great 'Lithgow Flash', Marjorie Jackson—having circumnavigated the Sydney Town Hall one night late in 1954 to secure her autograph at the annual ABC 'Sportsman of the Year' award.

Betty's first event was the 100 metres. Marlene Mathews, with a slightly better record and more experience, was the favourite to win. And there was serious competition from overseas: Christa Stubnick, a typist with the German police force, and Isabelle Daniels from America.

GLORIA COOKE It was very exciting because I had two friends from my club, Western Suburbs, in the race. Although Betty and Marlene had been running very well, there was speculation the German and American sprinters were the favourites.

But I don't think any of us knew what to expect in 1956. We hoped that we would do well since we were in our home country. But we were very innocent in those days. We didn't have many trips away for competition. The furthest afield most of us travelled before Melbourne would have been over to New Zealand.

In the first round of heats, Betty streaked home to beat the Olympic record in 11.4 seconds, but relaxed a little in the semi-finals and came in second behind Stubnick. She learned a valuable lesson from this, and didn't ease up for a split second in the final. 'I got away quickly and was stunned over the first 50 metres to find Daniels, who was two lanes away, breathing right down my neck', she said. 'She really made me go. I didn't think she'd be so much in the picture, but there she was, hanging on like grim death, and I had to really flatten myself to shake her off. I was so engrossed in getting rid of the American girl that my mind was taken off Marlene and Stubnick and, in fact, I never ever caught a glance of them any time during the race'.

With her trademark wide open mouth—'I thought my jaws were going to split'—Betty hit the line first in 11.5 seconds. It was Australia's first gold medal of the Games.

Only a few metres separate the six finalists in the 100 metres as they cross the finish line. From left: American Isabelle Daniels (who finished fourth), Italy's Giuseppina Leone (fifth), Australia's Betty Cuthbert (first) and Marlene Mathews (third), Britain's Heather Armitage (sixth) and German Christa Stubnick (second). AAP/AP PHOTO/GOPA

Black and white television, brand new in Australia in 1956, beamed images of her victory right across the country. And in that instant, she became the nation's darling, although she admits that the enormity of just what she had accomplished didn't really strike her at the time.

'Mum must have realised what I had done because I looked up in the crowd just after the race was over and saw her crying her eyes out', says Betty.

Stubnick pushed up into second place in 11.7 seconds, while a disappointed Marlene Mathews got up in a photo-finish with Daniels for the bronze medal in the same time.

MARLENE MATHEWS I pulled a hamstring muscle about a month before the Games. Then I contracted German measles about 10 days before we moved into the Village. None of the officials knew. But I was clear of it when I went into the Village.

The 100 metres was my favourite event. My form was OK in the lead-up. I won my heat and my semi-final. By rights, if I had got a reasonable start, I should have won the final. But I didn't, it was a dreadful start. I shudder every time I see film of it. Given wherever I was at the 50 metres mark, it was just good that I was able to come home and get the bronze medal.

I guess that I lost concentration. I used to always run better in my second race of the day. We had the heats and semi-finals on the Saturday. So it was a straight out final on the Monday. I was never a very good starter but that was probably my worst.

If I had a fairy godmother and she said I could have one thing in my life over again, I would like to run the final of the 100 metres in Melbourne. That's all. But then again, if I had won an Olympic gold medal, what would it have done for me? It probably would have got me more invites to dinners and lunches.

Their medals were presented by Hugh Weir, Australia's delegate to the IOC, who had been offered the task by the president, Avery Brundage. Betty received her gold medal in front of more than 90,000 cheering fans.

That night, in the Village dining hall, an exuberant Australian team celebrated in typical mid-fifties style. There was a big iced sponge cake, decorated with a gold medal and 'Congratulations'. And toasts were drunk to Betty Cuthbert—in orange juice.

The next day in the Village, Betty met the Prime Minister, Robert Menzies, and Governor-General, Sir William Slim, while media photographers clamoured to take photos of all three of them together. Later, the Prime Minister gave Betty a lift to the main stadium, where she watched Shirley Strickland win gold in the 80 metres hurdles in world record time.

For the unassuming, quietly determined girl from Ermington, life would never be the same.

Young Betty looks the part, modelling the Australian uniform for the Melbourne Games. BETTY CUTHBERT PERSONAL COLLECTION

top left: *Betty receives her gold medal from Hugh Weir, Australia's delegate to the International Olympic Committee.* THE HERALD & WEEKLY TIMES PHOTOGRAPHIC COLLECTIONS

top centre: *Betty is carried by her father Les and older brother John.* THE HERALD & WEEKLY TIMES PHOTOGRAPHIC COLLECTIONS

top right: *A win for the ages: Betty celebrates with her parents and friends, including bronze medallist Marlene Mathews.* THE HERALD & WEEKLY TIMES PHOTOGRAPHIC COLLECTIONS

bottom: *Betty Cuthbert, Christa Stubnick and Marlene Mathews finished 1–2–3 in both the women's 100 metres and 200 metres in Melbourne—the only time this has occurred at an Olympics Games.* NEWSPIX

opposite: *Australian Prime Minister Robert Menzies proudly escorts the darling of the track while the press photographers furiously try to capture the .moment.* THE HERALD & WEEKLY TIMES PHOTOGRAPHIC COLLECTIONS

top: *An enthusiastic press corps hangs on every word of Australia's newest sprinting sensation, Betty Cuthbert.* THE HERALD & WEEKLY TIMES PHOTOGRAPHIC COLLECTIONS

bottom left: *Prime Minister Robert Menzies, Betty and Governor-General Sir William Slim.* THE HERALD & WEEKLY TIMES PHOTOGRAPHIC COLLECTIONS

bottom right: *Six weeks earlier, his daughter was working in the family nursery. Now, Les Cuthbert tunes into the 1956 Olympics on his radio to listen to her brilliant run.* NEWSPIX

This is how *The Age* newspaper of 27 November 1956 reported her win.

LITHE TEENAGER OUR FIRST GOLD MEDALLIST

In a scatter of cinders and sawdust, one world record and four Olympic records were shattered at the Main Stadium yesterday.

But the records were small things to Australian eyes, which saw only a tousle-haired teenager named Betty Cuthbert, 18 years of age, and—since 5.21 pm yesterday—the fastest woman in the world.

The tense minutes before, and the joyous minutes after, the women's 100 metres final were as emotional as any the Games have provided.

Every Australian in the stadium—and there were close to 100,000 of them—seemed to share the weight of responsibility that belonged to Betty Cuthbert and Marlene Mathews.

They sat down to lace their running spikes and countless pairs of worried eyes followed every movement of their hands.

Once, Betty Cuthbert appeared to trip on the kerb of the track. Calamity coloured the sighs of all who saw it.

YARD AHEAD OF THE FIELD

In the event, it was just the crack of the starter's pistol, a thankfully brief period of tension and a blonde head a yard ahead of the field. We need not have worried at all.

The enormous crash of sound that ran through the Stadium might have been tempered with regret that Marlene Mathews had come only third.

But Miss Mathews was so quick to congratulate her faster team-mate that the crowd took its tone from her and shouted its pride and joy.

Miss Cuthbert was all smiles. She waved just once to a person hidden in the stands. It was her mother.

She walked back down the track to the start and the smiles were replaced by tears; lots of them.

It was altogether too much for a mere girl. She cried for a long time.

She was a little nervous and is not yet accustomed to fame—and acts it. Also, she seems the sort of girl who will always be that way.

Four days after the 100 metres, the 200 metres began. Betty easily won her heat and then her semi-final, this time with her coach, June Ferguson, watching from the grandstands. For the final the next day, June's advice to Betty (who was in lane five) was to catch Stubnick (outside her in lane six), before completing the curve into the straight, to make absolutely certain of winning.

That's precisely what happened. Betty won gold again, equalling the Olympic record of 23.4 seconds, once again ahead of Stubnick (23.7 seconds) and Marlene (23.8 seconds). For the first and only time in Olympic history, the medallists in the two sprints had finished in the exact same order. With Norma Croker fourth, Australia filled three of the first four places.

MARLENE MATHEWS I used to win my 200 metres at interclub, but I never had a lot of confidence over the distance. In those days, you used to relax a bit going around the bend and then you would come home at the end. After the disappointment of the 100 metres, I thought, 'I've got to improve my performance'. So I was quite happy with the bronze medal.

Once again, the Australian crowd roared as the medals were presented. And the entire front page of Melbourne's *The Argus* was devoted to a glorious coloured action photograph of Betty. Down the side ran the simple caption: 'Betty Cuthbert—Golden Girl'. Betty was stunned, overwhelmed—and as the phrase quickly swelled to an adoring catch-cry, she caught a tiny glimpse of the impact her dual win would have over the weeks, months and years to come.

The Argus is long since defunct, but Betty still receives mail addressed simply to 'The Golden Girl, Australia'. And public functions still erupt into applause as soon as they hear her introduced. Although 'Golden Girl' is now a term of adulation frequently applied to outstanding sportswomen, none has ever outshone the original: Betty Cuthbert.

opposite: *With arms and legs 'pumping like mad', Betty stretches to victory in the women's 200 metres final ahead of the German, Christa Stubnick.*
THE HERALD & WEEKLY TIMES
PHOTOGRAPHIC COLLECTIONS

For the first and only time in Olympic history, the medallists in the two sprints had finished in the exact same order.

Betty's winning time of 23.4 seconds is recorded on the MCG scoreboard. While the time is an Olympic record, it is actually 0.2 seconds slower than the world record she set in Sydney two months earlier. THE HERALD & WEEKLY TIMES PHOTOGRAPHIC COLLECTION

One person's pleasure is another's pain: Betty lunges towards victory in the 100 metres. Marlene Mathews, who took the bronze medal, says the race is her biggest regret in life. It also cost her a place in the 4x100 metres relay. THE HERALD & WEEKLY TIMES PHOTOGRAPHIC COLLECTION

IAN HEADS   My seats in Melbourne were on the far side of the track from the finishing line (for reasons not unconnected to money, I would imagine)—but the view I had of Betty remains keenly imprinted on my mind. The image of her at the tape—white top, green shorts—is long since an iconic one in Australia's memory and the country's pictorial history: a champion in full flight, her head back, her mouth open as she gulps in the air. A few years later, it seemed to me that the peerless rugby league centre Reg Gasnier would throw his head back at just that angle when he put his foot to the floor.

On the blue-skied Melbourne days of that long ago November, I cheered Betty's progress through the rounds of the 100 and 200 metres—and then rose with the mob as she gloriously won both finals. In the newspapers, she was instantly our 'Golden Girl'. And she was … and is … and will be, forever. Germany's Christa Stubnick split 'our girls' Betty and Marlene to take silver in both the sprints. But my recall is that the cheers for Marlene Mathews were just as they were for Betty. Melbourne loved her equally.

For Betty, there was still the 4x100 metres relay to contest. But attention was diverted from the Golden Girl's quest for her third gold medal by controversy surrounding the selectors' choice of the relay team.

Instead of selecting Marlene Mathews as runner number three, they chose Fleur Mellor, apparently considering her a better option because she was a proven relay runner and was fresher than Marlene and Gloria Cooke. With Shirley Strickland, Norma Croker, Fleur and Betty, the team were definite race favourites. But the selection of Fleur was hotly debated, and sympathy ran high for Marlene who, it was argued, deserved another shot at gold after demonstrating in both the 100 and 200 metres finals that she was the third fastest woman in the world.

MARLENE MATHEWS   Probably the biggest disappointment I've ever had was being left out of the women's 4x100 metres relay. There were various theories. One was that I wasn't a very good starter and the 100 metres final provided reasonable doubt. But the selectors could have put me somewhere else in the relay.

And it was said I couldn't run a bend, yet I had just picked up the bronze medal in the 200 metres. I think it was politics.

It might have been less painful if they gave me a reason. Back in those days, we didn't question the selectors. You accepted what they said and that was it. It was great to see the girls win and pick up a gold medal, but that didn't ease my disappointment. Melbourne was a bittersweet experience for me.

It must have been an extremely difficult decision. Perhaps it would have been debated no matter what the final line-up was.

GLORIA COOKE I had finished sixth in the 80 metres hurdles won by Shirley Strickland, and hoped that I would be chosen in the 4x100 metres relay team. In those days, Marlene, Betty and I raced together at interclub meetings every Saturday afternoon in our athletic season. We won many state championships for Western Suburbs. You would have been led to think the selectors would leave part of the combination there. But that wasn't to be, and Marlene and I weren't selected.

A gold for Australia in the relay was by no means a forgone conclusion. So there was great excitement when, pressed by the Germans in the opening heat, the Australian team set a world record of 44.9 seconds. In the final, it was the British who applied the pressure. At the last change, Heather Armitage and Betty Cuthbert took the batons almost simultaneously and the Golden Girl put in a mighty effort to edge ahead just before the tape. The time flashed up: 44.5 seconds—another world record. And a third gold medal for Betty Cuthbert.

Britain clocked 44.7 seconds, and the United States finished third in 44.9. One member of the American team was a young 'unknown', Wilma Rudolph who, four years later in Rome, would emulate Betty by winning both sprints and the relay.

JUDY PATCHING Betty was an unknown quantity prior to the final of the 100 metres. From the Australian public's point of view, Marlene Mathews was the better runner. However, by the final of the 4x100 metres relay, everybody had realised Betty Cuthbert was a great performer and the interest was very intense.

Shirley Strickland had won the 80 metres hurdles, so we had a couple of gold medallists in the relay team. The selectors didn't pick Marlene Mathews. Instead they chose Fleur Mellor, which was extraordinary.

The fact that Betty had won the 100 metres and the 200 metres didn't mean our relay team was a certainty to win. The tension reached its peak with everybody watching Betty, who finished the relay as the final runner. The elation was fantastic when their time was announced as a world record.

Betty Cuthbert's name is etched in Australian folklore as she passes Great Britain's Heather Armitage on the last leg of the women's 4x100 metres relay final. The Australian team's gold medal winning time of 44.5 seconds is a new world record.

THE HERALD & WEEKLY TIMES
PHOTOGRAPHIC COLLECTION

The 1956 Melbourne Olympic Games were all over for Betty. In the nine glorious days that ended on 1 December 1956, she won three gold medals and twice shared in breaking world records. She was the first Australian, male or female, of a small select group ever to win three gold medals at a single Olympics. (The others are Murray Rose—1956; Shane Gould—1972; and Ian Thorpe—2000.)

But Betty, with her sweet naivety, distinctive style and fabulous wins, had etched herself into the nation's sporting history as the Golden Girl. Australia, along with the rest of the developed world, was on the verge of dramatic technological and social change. In some sense, the Golden Girl embodied the final glow of a fading era, not only in sport, but in many aspects of society and culture.

IAN HEADS The Melbourne Games marked the end of innocence in world sport. There was a sense that a great warmth and generous spirit circulated around and through those Games. The cheers for those in green and gold seemed entirely about affection and pride—light years removed from the ugly flag-waving jingoism/nationalism that crept into Australian sporting crowds in later years. There was generous appreciation for those from other places. Back then such things as professionalism, rampant commercialism and the heavy, throttling hand of the media on sport were still a few years away. For all that, the reality that politics and sport were not so far apart—with the gap closing fast—surfaced dramatically, even in Melbourne's warm glow, notably in a bruising water polo match between Hungary and Russia which spawned a famous photo of a Hungarian player leaving the pool, blood pouring down his face. Amidst all the goodwill, the Cold War and the realities of the modern world had come to town.

Back at school in Sydney, I had a further taste of this encroaching world feeling not long after getting home. In a 2E Maths class at Sydney Boys High I was invited to talk to my classmates of some of my experiences at the Games. I began rashly by recounting the deeds of the Russian sailor Kuts, whose relentless stop–start tactics in both the 5000 and 10,000 metres broke the hearts and the spirit of his English rivals. Both races had been enthralling spectacles. But the teacher cut me short. 'We've heard enough about the Russian', he snapped.

opposite: *Action from the Olympics is front page news in* The Herald, *although the main headline—'Pretty Betty Wins Our Gold Medal'—is indicative of an era when political correctness was not a sensitive issue.* THE HERALD & WEEKLY TIMES PHOTOGRAPHIC COLLECTION

The Herald

Registered in Australia for transmission by post as a newspaper

No. 24,804   MELBOURNE, the Olympic City, MONDAY, NOV. 26, 1956   Phones: MF0211   24 PAGES   **3d.**

PRETTY BETTY WINS OUR 4th GOLD MEDAL

Herald Staff Reporter

Australia won her first Gold Medal of the 1956 Olympic Games at the Olympic Stadium this afternoon.

Before a madly cheering, waving crowd of more than 90,000 people, pretty Betty Cuthbert, 18, flashed home first in the final of the women's 100 metres.

Unrestrained cheering, shouting, whistling and stamping of feet broke out.

Less than 12 seconds earlier the crowd and stadium had been silent. As the six girl finalists got down on their marks it was the moment the crowd had been waiting for all day.

All previous events were just "preliminaries."

There was a photo finish for second place.

And Marlene Mathews filled third place to give Australia another bronze medal.

Betty's time was   sec. This is 0.1 seconds outside her own Olympic record which she set yesterday.

☛ **Soviet arms Syria, P. 7**

And here's other headline news inside The Herald today.

PAGE 2: Mons. Tipping sees the fencing in Black and White.

PAGE 3: The Games in pictures.

PAGE 5: Prisoner escape sequel — girl committed for trial; Power step threat.

● And in the back section of The Herald you'll find other Olympic news and pictures.

Marlene Mathews (left) and Betty Cuthbert photographed to-day before Australia's first Gold Medal.

HERALD OLYMPIC RECORD

THE HERALD'S circulation soared to record figures on Friday and Saturday to satisfy interest in the Olympic Games.

Never before have so many Heralds been printed.

Here are the figures:—

Friday   537,115
Saturday   531,498

The Sun News-Pictorial also broke circulation records on Friday and Saturday. On those days it printed 533,639 and 522,365 copies.

This means that well over a million Heralds and Suns were printed daily.

100 METRES

(Continued from Back Page)

After a hold-up of about eight minutes the placings were announced.

The American girl Daniels waited up the arena, evidently expecting that she would be in the first three placings for the victory ceremony.

Cuthbert meanwhile was in the race leading to the dressing-room.

Daniels appeared crestfallen when she heard that Stubnick had taken second place, and she herself had not been placed in the first three.

Cuthbert burst into tears when she heard the official announcement that she had become a gold medallist.

POLE VAULT

Left in at 14ft. 11¼in. R. Gutowski (USA), R. E. Richards (USA.)

JAVELIN

Six competitors left in after three rounds: J. Sidlo (Poland), 263 ft. 5 in. (betters Olympic record); V. Tsiboulenko (Russia), 248 ft. 10 in. (betters Olympic record); M. Koschel (Germany), 246 ft.; J. Kopyto (Poland); G. Lievore (Italy); E. Danielsen (Norway).

HOCKEY

Group B

Australia 3 d. Malaya 1. — Goal-hitters: Australia, Eric Pearce, Mel Pearce (2); Malaya, Kartin. Best players: Australia, Spackman, Mel Pearce, Whiteside; Malaya: Shanmugamatham, Kartin.

BASKETBALL

GROUP C

Uruguay d Korea 83-60.

U.S. star wins 800-metre thriller

America's tally of Gold Medals increased today and more Olympic records were shattered.

Tom Courtney, 23, of America, won the 800 metres final in a thrilling finish at the Stadium. He beat Britain's D. Johnson after a stirring struggle over the last 70 yards.

United States, hopeful of filling the first three places, was also beaten for third place by Norwegian A. Boysen.

The Olympic record of 1 min. 49.2 secs. set up by M. Whitfield (U.S.) in 1948, was beaten by Courtney, Johnson, Boysen and Sowell (U.S.).

The crowd went wild when little Alan Lawrence beat Soviet star Vladimir Kuts by five yards in his heat of the 5000 metres.

Lawrence won a bronze medal for Australia when he ran third to Kuts in the 10,000 metres event last Friday.

Crept through

Today Lawrence followed leader Kuts until one and a half laps from home when he crept through on the inside.

The two raced shoulder to shoulder until the final turn when Lawrence eased away and went on to win by five yards.

Kuts appeared to have a lot in reserve. Australia's A. Thomas also won his heat.

There were special cheers, too, for heat winner, Gordon Pirie, of Britain.

Cool days — Bureau

Melbourne seems assured of at least two more days of fine Olympic weather.

Temperatures — in the 60s today—were below average and there were periods of cloud.

The Weather Bureau says tomorrow should be finer and slightly warmer. Temperatures may be appreciably higher on Wednesday.

Since the Games began on Thursday, Melbourne has not registered a single point of rain.

TOM COURTNEY (U.S.) spurts to the tape to score a brilliant victory in the 800 metres final from D. J. N. Johnson (Britain) and A. Boysen (Norway) at the Main Stadium this afternoon.

Kuts down to Australia

Long lead

The crowd remembered his gallant but vain efforts to match Kuts in the 10,000 metres last Friday.

Today, Pirie streaked away to a long lead, but showed almost to a walk in the straight and went across the finish line with his arm around V. Mugosa of Yugoslavia.

Another Gold Medal went to America when Tommy Kono won the weightlifting heavy-weight with a world record total lift of 447.5 Kilogrammes (986.25 lbs.) at the Exhibition Building.

At Lake Wendouree the Australia eight qualified for the finals. The crew was just beaten by America.

Hogan cheered

Australian Hec Hogan was cheered as he got down on his mark for his 200 metres heat, and as he finished second easing up behind Czech runner V. Mandlik.

Hogan seemed content merely to qualify.

The crowd laughed and cheered as only two runners fought out the sixth heat of the 200 metres.

K. Akagi (Japan) and J. Machado de Barros (Brazil) were the only starters in their heat. But they made a race of it.

The three American representatives in the 200 metres — Olympic record holder A. W. Stanfield, 100 metres winner Bob Morrow, and 100 metres silver medallist Thane Baker—each 'won their heats with almost nonchalant ease.

High fliers

While the 200 metres sprint stars whirled half way round the brick-red track, another group of athletes in front of the score board drew gasps of admiration.

They were the 14 finalists in the pole vault.

an event which has been won by the United States since the modern Games started in 1896.

America's strong trio in the event this year includes 1953 winner and Olympic record holder, the Rev. Robert E. Richards — known popularly in America as "the Flying Pastor."

Richards, a 30-year-old father of three children, is the second man in the world to vault more than 15 feet.

Victor Tsiboulenko (Russia) this afternoon shattered the new Olympic javelin record set by American cowboy Cy Young earlier.

At his first throw this afternoon Tsiboulenko registered 240 ft. 11 in., bettering Young's record by 6 in.

Australia's two representatives, J. Achurch and R. Grant, failed to qualify.

A brisk wind was blowing almost directly up the 100 metres track. It bothered athletes and caused officials trouble.

First, they had to adjust the flagpole carrying the Japanese flag on top of the outer concrete stand.

Later a strong gust of wind blew down the Olympic flag fluttering from a 70 ft. high pole near the scoreboard end of the stadium.

U.S. leads

Before the women's 100-metre final the unofficial points count (U.S. style) showed U.S. 126, leading Russia, which scored U.S. 120, Australia, 19, in sixth place.

The European - style count gives U.S. 109, Russia 84 and Australia (6th) 19.

SHIELD CRICKET

NSW v. WEST AUST.

West. Australia 2nd inns.
Simpson, not out   88
Bugess, not out   30
Extras   8

Seven wickets for 142 (Stumps)

Bowling: Crawford 0 22, Davidson 2 42, Treanor 2 51, Benaud 2 53, Martin 1 16.

AUSTRALIA'S Allan Lawrence dashing across the line to win his heat of the 5000-metres this afternoon — from Russia's Vladimir Kuts, hero of last Friday's 10,000 metres race.

Tatts details, Page 17

So, I talked instead that morning of Betty Cuthbert of Ermington, Sydney and of how wonderfully she had run and won, and how fortunate I felt to have been there.

It remains, 50 years on, as one of the sweetest of memories in a life spent chronicling branches of sport's world. Among my souvenirs, I still have the Melbourne Games track and field programs, with results carefully noted in a boyish hand: 'Cuthbert 1, Stubnick 2, Mathews 3'.

HERB ELLIOTT It was an incredibly mind-blowing experience for me as an 18-year-old Western Australian to go across to Melbourne with my parents and watch the 1956 Olympics. I had never been to Melbourne at that stage. It was a huge city in relation to Perth ... The Olympic Opening Ceremony was magnificent, seeing the various country names written on tracksuits and people with different coloured skins.

A group portrait of 38 gold medal winners at Melbourne's 'Friendly Games', featuring Australia's stars of the track and pool, Betty Cuthbert and Dawn Fraser. NATIONAL LIBRARY OF AUSTRALIA

As a spectator in the stands of the MCG, I was in awe of the god-like athletes that a skinny fellow like me could only wish to emulate. Two people, in particular, affected me most. The first was Vladimir Kuts, the Soviet sailor. I drew inspiration from the remorseless manner in which he beat the world's best over 5000 metres and 10,000 metres.

Betty Cuthbert was the other great influence, especially as I was just two months older than her. Betty's wins were unbelievable. We were so used to people from other nationalities winning the sprints. For her to win the three gold medals was very inspiring. I still remember the crowd roaring and the great pride we felt as the Australian flag went up on the occasions of Betty's wins.

With three gold medals, Betty showed me that Aussies could beat the almighty Europeans and Americans. In those days, Australians had a huge inferiority complex with regard to Europe and America. That obviously didn't bother her one iota. Her performances in Melbourne certainly removed any thoughts that you may ever have had that Australians couldn't be as good as anybody else. She removed an obstacle in my mind before my career had started.

MIKE AGOSTINI Betty captured the imagination of the Australian public for the same reason as Don Bradman. When you have someone who can beat the world, like Don Bradman did in cricket, they become heroes. This is especially so when you have a nation that feels put down, as was the case with Australia—the little sister, and England—the big sister. More so, in a country that is small and isolated. In the 1950s, a trip to Australia by propeller planes took almost a week from Europe.

Decima Norman won five gold medals in the 1938 Empire [now Commonwealth] Games in Sydney. But she never had the personality to capture people's imagination. Then along came Marjorie Jackson and she was the best in the world over 100 metres and 200 metres. But Marj didn't quite have the personality or Betty's good looks.

'With three gold medals, Betty showed me that Aussies could beat the almighty Europeans and Americans.'

HERB ELLIOTT

The Australian
WOMEN'S WEEKLY

Over 750,000 Copies Sold Every Week

Registered in Australia for transmission by post as a newspaper.

December 12, 1956

PRICE
9

AUSTRALIA'S
WONDERFUL GIRLS

69

MIKE AGOSTINI Betty was a bright, pert, beautiful woman with blue eyes and curly blonde hair. To a then racist, Anglophile, Anglo-Saxon nation, that was so important. Betty had the perfect personality. She was shy. She was sweet. She was lovely. She didn't smoke, she wouldn't drink. She didn't even have a boyfriend. To an Australia of that time, the mid-1950s, Betty was the perfect person.

She is an example of how racial and cultural icons are stereotyped into the Australian psyche. But make no mistake about it, she deserved the attention because she was a fantastic athlete. She is still the only person, male or female, ever to win the 100 metres, 200 metres and 400 metres at the Olympics. And she set a collection of world records. Marlene Mathews was great in 1958 and held world records for 100 yards, 220 yards, and 440 yards. But she wasn't a patch on Betty. Betty beat the world at home and there's nothing quite like it.

Prior to the Melbourne Olympics, Australia was a white man's country. That isn't said in a derogatory manner; it's just the way it was. It was incredibly racist, but not in a South African sense. I don't think there was a single Indian restaurant in Australia in 1956; there were Chinese restaurants that were usually run by Greeks. But the Olympics changed Australia immensely. The Melbourne food improved because the Italian, and some of the Greek, chefs came back out here to live. Those types of influences brought Australia into the rest of the world.

I think that Melbourne was the last of the good old Games. And Sydney might well be the last of the big Games because I don't know what's going to happen to the world. So it might well be that Australia has the pleasure and privilege of having hosted the last of the great Games.

Clearly, world politics and 1950s Australian culture played their part in ensuring that such an intense spotlight shone on Betty Cuthbert. But the fond recollections of many of her peers make it clear that there was more to it. An almost indefinable golden quality—quite aside from her winning of gold medals—seemed, even then, to set Betty apart from her team-mates.

RON CLARKE   Apart from being a triple gold medallist, Betty captured the attention of the Australian public in 1956 because she was young. Everything about her was charismatic. Even if Marlene Mathews had been on form and won, I don't know whether she would have got the same attention as Betty. It's not as if Marlene wasn't a sweet person. But Betty was a different type of person. She was very straightforward, but quite innocent, very honest and down to earth.

BRUCE McAVANEY   The whole story of Betty in Melbourne was so heart-warming. She gave us those unforgettable images with her mouth wide open, winning the 100 metres and the 200 metres, and then being part of the relay team that gave her a third gold medal. I love the humbleness of her going to Melbourne—from the surprise of being able to make the Australian team and then absolutely soaring to the greatest heights.

I've spoken to Betty a lot over the years. I remember her telling me that she didn't expect to be in Melbourne and had organised some tickets for her parents, although her father wasn't able to come down from Sydney because of commitments at the family's nursery. After winning the 100 metres, Betty says she looked up into the stands and saw her mother crying. That family link makes me very emotional. Here she was on a world stage, and the most important thing to her was not that public adulation. It was the realisation that she had done something that was moving, not only for the whole country, but also for the parents that she loved.

DAVID PRINCE   Betty was the girl next door. There's no doubt about that. Her popularity at the Melbourne Olympics was unbelievable. She won the hearts of every Australian. She was so humble and handled herself so well that she was almost apologetic.

I can still hear the roar of the crowd in Melbourne, because it was for her. This little girl from the nursery, 18 years of age, with qualities that Australia has become renowned for in our female swimmers. Jodie Henry would be a good comparison today. Jodie came out of the blue a little bit. She has a beautiful smile and a wholesome image. And Betty was that in 1956.

I can still see the photographs of Betty on the front pages of all the newspapers—— this little 18-year-old girl meeting the Duke of Edinburgh, the Prime Minister Robert Menzies, and all of these dignitaries. The Duke just had to meet this great young lady who, the week before, was pulling weeds in her Dad's nursery.

Humble, sweet, down to earth. And with a distinctive running style that not even June Ferguson had been able to coach into conformity. Betty's contemporaries comment over and over again on this.

DAVID PRINCE Fanny Blankers-Koen and Marjorie Jackson were the two great women sprinters before Betty. They were smooth runners, whereas Betty was an aggressive runner. Betty's technique was very efficient and one of the features was a fantastically high knee lift, which no other woman sprinter had in that era. With a very high knee lift and an arm action that was pumping like mad, Betty might have been the first of the aggressive women sprinters.

GLORIA COOKE Most champions aren't exactly copybook. Tennis players and other champion sportsmen all put their own personal stamp on their success. Betty had her own unique style of running. She used to lift her knees and throw her feet out. If I close my eyes, I can still picture Betty's stride in my mind.

RON CLARKE Of all the sprinters I've seen, I wouldn't say Betty was the prettiest. But she was very effective. All sorts of styles win all sorts of races. I've heard experts say there's no way somebody could win with a certain running style and the person has done it easily. The main thing is to get over the ground as quickly as you can and Betty managed to do that very well.

MIKE AGOSTINI   Betty had great natural speed and great knee lift. Her parents come from New Zealand and New Zealand breeds great racehorses! …The reason for her success is that she's a competitor. Behind that sweet, soft side is a calm, confident, capable person. In my opinion, her mission in life was to become a great sprinter. She was the greatest sprinter of her time and the greatest all-round sprinter that Australia has ever had.

Considering the uniforms the women had to wear in those days, that's quite a claim. They were certainly not assisted by stream-lined aerodynamic body suits.

MARLENE MATHEWS   Our uniforms were really antique. You could describe our shorts as Bombay bloomers. I remember asking permission to thread elastic through the legs, so that we could pull them up a bit. We even had to kneel down on the ground to make sure that the shorts were a certain distance above our knees. And it was: 'Tuck your shirt in' or you were disqualified. It was ridiculous. I could never imagine us running in bikinis, which they virtually do now.

Marlene, Norma and Betty unite for a group hug after the women's 200 metres final. The trio had filled three of the top four places in a race against Europe's best—German pair Gisela Kohler and Christa Stubnick (left), plus Great Britain's June Paul (centre).

NORMA CROKER   We had Bombay bloomer pants with legs like parachute wings. And they were made of hard, stiff material. Shirley [Strickland] said we should have softer fabrics. But we couldn't be too cheeky. So they made another batch of shorts and we put a bit of fine elastic in the legs, which just made them like little bloomer pants. When we saw some of the overseas athletes, we thought, 'Boy, we are still years behind the times as far as running gear'.

GLORIA COOKE   Our pants were ghastly. The rule was, if you were to kneel on the floor, the officials would measure seven inches [18 centimetres] up your leg. Your pants weren't to be any shorter than that. If you were a hurdler, there's no way you could pull your leg up and put it over a hurdle. So my Mum used to put elastic around the bottom of my shorts, so that I could pull them up. It was just old fashioned. When you look at the stuff they wear these days, the dress regulations seem to have gone from the sublime to the ridiculous.

Not all the young women on the team went home bearing medals. But for many of those who competed, the Melbourne Games served as a right of passage; a transformational life experience. They hailed from all over Australia, bonded by outstanding athletic skills, determination, dedication and a desire to compete for their country at the highest sporting level. And for many, knowing Betty Cuthbert, training with her, sharing living quarters, and helping celebrate her sensational successes added unanticipated warmth and affection to their enduring memories.

NORMA CROKER   The first time I met Betty would have been Easter 1956 when she came up to Brisbane for the Australian national championships. They were the first ones that I ever ran in, partly because they were held every two years. It was a big moment with the Olympics later in the year and so we were allowed to compete on the Gabba, although it was a quagmire when we eventually ran.

My preparation wasn't ideal for the 200 metres. I hadn't been very well, apart from the fact that I hadn't done any training. I had been teaching up bush and had nowhere to run. I was at a little one-teacher school and being billeted on a farm just outside Beaudesert in the Gold Coast hinterland. I had to ride my pushbike to and from school. There was no public transport and I didn't have a car. A lot of people didn't. I was dependent on one of the other young teachers working at another school a few miles away. If he was going home to Brisbane for the weekend, he would pick me up and drop me back at Lloyd's place on the way home on Friday so that I could compete on the Saturday at the club.

Anyway, I got the program and who do I draw in the heat but Marlene Mathews. I had been keeping company with Lloyd for a while and he said, 'I tell you what, if you beat her we'll get engaged'. And I did. Every time Lloyd sees Marlene, he says, 'Norma paid you to run dead'.

The nationals was the first time I met Shirley Strickland, who was there with the Western Australian team. I idolised Shirley: every sporting magazine had stories about her. She came up to me after my run and said, 'Good run, lass. A bit more hard work and you could go far'. I had no idea that a few months down the track she would be handing me the baton in the relay final. So I took Shirley's advice and ran well enough at the final trials to win a spot in the team for the Games.

Although I finished second in my qualifying heat and third in a semi-final, I didn't give myself much of a chance in the 200 metre final. I didn't have a coach in those days, nor did I know how to prepare properly. And Melbourne was so out of reach for me, coming from little Brisbane town. I had rarely been out of Queensland, so it was quite a big deal to compete in Melbourne.

Even though some of the German girls had very fast times leading into the Games, we realised Betty was a strong chance to win the final after the way she ran in the 100 metres. Home crowd support and running in the right season gave her an advantage, too.

I was happy for Betty and Marlene, who edged me out for the bronze medal. Looking back, I think I just ran out of puff. I wasn't fully prepared to run a heat, a semi and a final. I don't have any regrets about it because I was absolutely thrilled to have made the final. But you don't get any accolades for fourth.

Congratulations for Betty and Marlene from Norma Croker, who admits she ran out of puff over the 200 metres. AUSTRALIAN CONSOLIDATED PRESS

I didn't get to know the other girls in the relay squad until 1956. Betty, Marlene Mathews, Fleur Mellor and Gloria Cooke all lived in Sydney. Shirley Strickland was in Perth and I was in Queensland. When we did go into the Olympic Village, we lived in these little housing commission homes. We slept in the same house, two or three to a room. I think the New South Wales girls would have been in one room and the Queenslanders in another. So there was no teamwork there until the relay.

We were treated like kids in Melbourne. The officials said you had to be in bed by 9 o'clock, so you went to bed at that time. There was no questioning it (except perhaps from the swimmers—I think they might have played a few tricks on their coaches). It took someone as mature as Shirley Strickland to question the managers. She could see that some of the things they were saying we should do were quite stupid.

•   •   •   •

The relay was the prime example of the stupidity. Relays are won on teamwork. And we really didn't know who was in the team. The officials were saying, 'We'll run you in different positions because we're going to confuse the press'. Of course, we were under close scrutiny from the press. If you think back further, it was the previous Olympics when the girls dropped the baton. And we weren't allowed to speak to the press. That was another rule.

Anyway, we were going to confuse the press, according to the official. She had us running in every position, which way but that. And it was only Shirley who spoke up and said, 'For heaven's sake, we're not confusing the press, you're confusing us. And unless we work out who's going to run in what order, we're the ones who are going to be confused'. It was only then that we were told what order we would run.

I had a lot of respect for Shirley. We needed somebody like her to speak sensibly to the officials. Betty was a rookie to the Games, the same as we were, whereas Shirley had previous experience from London and Helsinki. She was very well respected in athletic fields because she had a real brain. She was a very clever woman.

[In the relay] Shirley started, and she handed the baton to me, then I gave it to Fleur Mellor and Fleur handed it on to Betty. You really do have to trust the person coming from behind in a relay. Then you've just got to go full bore and hope you connect with the next runner before you pass the front box. That, of course, is something that goes through your mind. You have a mark where you've got to take off and you put all of your trust in the person handing you the baton. I suppose Betty put all of her trust in God—Fleur was going to catch her before she reached that front marker.

It was a very close finish but it was terribly exciting. Of course, once you've done your bit, you're just standing there watching the other girls. Betty ran a brilliant last leg. It was terrific. I think the English girl may have been a little bit ahead at the last baton change and Betty mowed her down. But it was very close. From where I was standing after my change, I had to wait for the result to come up on the electronic scoreboard to know that Betty had got there safely.

I can't remember any celebrations after we won the relay. We were probably told we had to go to bed at 8 o'clock! I think the relay was on the last day of the track and field competition. So everyone would have been free and easy. But there were no grand celebrations. The security was a double-whammy. The men weren't allowed anywhere near our sleeping quarters. It was very tame. The Village was magnificent as far as we were concerned, but there were no games rooms or discos or entertainment areas. It was purely our accommodation and the dining area.

The overseas teams, with their close proximity to one another when they were at home, had a lot more international competition than we did. We didn't travel anywhere to compete, except interstate, which was rare. To think we had a first, a third and a fourth in the 200 metres. In the 100 metres we had a first and a third. In the 80 metres hurdles we had a first, a third and a sixth. Then we won the 4x100 metres relay. So the Australian women sprinters didn't do too badly. There were only four races for women in 1956. We won all four and collected seven of the 12 medals on the track.

Television had just arrived in Australia by the time of the Melbourne Olympics, although it was only black and white. You would see groups of people standing outside electrical shops watching the shows through the window. It was amazing.

• • • •

So in 1956, much of the public's perception of sportspeople would have been through pictorial spreads in the press. As a public, we like the looks of people as well as what they achieve. And Betty was a good, clean-living, honest young woman, as I felt we all were in those days. She didn't do anything that put a smear against her name. She was the blonde, pretty little athlete of the day.

Betty said she had a God-given gift to run. I quite agree with her on that. But she certainly used it and trained terribly hard. I think she was very focused. She also had a supportive family—she was able to work for her dad in the nursery. And Betty had a wonderful coach in June Ferguson, who spotted her talent when she was at primary school and fostered it. So she was very fortunate in that regard.

She led a natural lifestyle, working in the open air. And she's always had that lovely fresh look about her: the golden hair and the bright smiley face.

Such extraordinary achievements. So much adulation. So many memories. But the last word must go to Betty Cuthbert, the original Golden Girl: 'It was the most wonderful week in my life.'

opposite: *Despite a controversial selection process and disrupted preparation, Fleur Mellor, Norma Croker, Betty Cuthbert and Shirley Strickland helped Australia to a clean sweep of the four women's sprints in Melbourne.* NATIONAL ARCHIVES OF AUSTRALIA

Triumph against the odds

Could Betty Cuthbert possibly win a fourth gold medal?

With three gold medals to her credit, Betty Cuthbert returned home to Ermington elated and exhausted, desperately wanting to relax, spend time with her family, and visit her new baby nephew, Stephen. But Sydney and Sydneysiders had other ideas. Intent on continuing the Melbourne celebrations, they were not going to let the Golden Girl and her team-mates slip away. Sydney feted the Olympic athletes with a ticker-tape parade, a civic reception and—later—a state reception. The first two weeks after their return passed in a blur of social and media engagements.

At the Cuthbert home, there was a never-ending stream of callers: the phone rarely stopped ringing, reporters and photographers came in droves, and telegrams, letters and flowers poured in. It took Betty more than a year to answer all her mail.

One little boy wrote to say his pet cow had given birth to calves: he'd called one 'Betty' and the other 'Cuthbert'. Someone else named his horse 'Olympic Betty'. Betty had a camellia named after her, and was depicted on a stamp in a commemorative series issued by the Dominican Republic in the West Indies—the first living Australian ever to appear on any stamp.

Tourist buses began stopping outside the house. Cars would drive past with the driver shouting out well-meaning greetings and congratulations.

In the midst of all this, a week after the Games finished, Betty lined up with her Melbourne team-mates to run two relays in the Australia versus USA versus the Commonwealth in Sydney. Shirley Strickland, Norma Croker, Fleur Mellor and Betty

Left, opposite and previous: *In the glow of Melbourne gold, Betty is welcomed home by throngs of well-wishers.*
AUSTRALIAN CONSOLIDATED PRESS

Cuthbert ran 45.6 seconds to break the 4x110 yards world record. Then, with Marlene Mathews replacing Shirley Strickland on the opening leg, the team won the 4x220 yards relay as well, setting a new world record of 1 minute 36.3 seconds. An adoring public lapped it up.

But Betty had lost her privacy, and felt at risk of losing her identity as well. She had become public property. 'My life wasn't my own any more', she recalls. And for a quiet, private person like Betty, the unrelenting spotlight was unnerving, to say the least. In those whirlwind final weeks of 1956, Betty—yearning to be left alone—even considered retiring, but felt duty-bound to continue, promising herself that the 1960 Rome Olympics would definitely mark the end of her athletics career. Having made her decision, Betty—in typical fashion—focused her full attention on training and competition.

GLORIA COOKE After 1956, we were all at the age when we were getting engaged. Both Marlene and I got engaged. Nancy Fogarty got engaged. Everybody was getting engaged. Bet used to say that she wasn't going to think about marriage until after she retired from athletics.

She thought that was the right thing to do because of the way we used to train four nights a week and compete every Saturday afternoon. Bet thought that it wasn't fair on a man to have to put up with that. She was very considerate of other people.

The glittering success of the Melbourne Games, extensively reported in the press and beamed across the nation via the exciting new medium of television, had heightened the Australian public's interest in sport, and Betty—inevitably—was one of the stars. Many other young athletes were swept along in the excitement as well.

DAVID PRINCE I rarely trained with Betty after 1956, although we would see each other three or four days a week at Epping Oval. I had started to run a lot faster once I got to 16 and was becoming a hurdler. But we would always warm up together.

Betty Cuthbert is about to take the baton from Fleur Mellor in the 4 x 110 yards relay to set a new world record of 45.6 seconds at the British Empire & Commonwealth v USA games in 1956. APA COLLECTION, MITCHELL LIBRARY, STATE LIBRARY OF NEW SOUTH WALES

In many respects, I was really carried away by the Melbourne Olympics as a young teenager. Betty was one of many people whom I idolised ... One of the great features of the lady was that she was so unaffected by it all. It would be interesting to see whether that would have occurred in today's terribly commercial world. Betty was so unaffected, almost bordering on naivety.

I honestly believe she endeared herself to people just by being natural. There was never any falsified part of her character. She was just a natural person who was gifted.

MARLENE MATHEWS   Betty became much more high profile after the Melbourne Olympics. Back in those days, Australia was pretty naive as far as sporting achievements were concerned. We only had television from 1956. I think Betty captured the imagination of the Australian public because she was so young and blonde.

GLORIA COOKE   Being the golden age of athletics, we used to get a lot of publicity in the newspapers. Rarely a day passed when you wouldn't grab the afternoon paper and open up the back pages to see who was in it. There were always stories about Betty and Marlene. Television had only just started then, so there wasn't as much hoo-ha via that medium. But we used to get an incredible amount of newspaper publicity.

Soon Betty was back into the grind of training and competition, and the wins continued. In 1957, she won her first New South Wales state title, running the 220 yards in 23.9 seconds, before travelling to New Zealand for a series of carnivals in which she won the 75, 100 and 220 yards championships. When her coach, June Ferguson, started up a new club—Cumberland—near Betty's home early in the 1957–58 season, Betty transferred her membership from Western Suburbs and trained harder than ever.

The healthy rivalry between Betty and Marlene was intense, and during 1957–58 the two gifted young runners battled it out on the track for personal and world bests in the 100 and 220 yards sprints. Both women were selected for the 1958 Cardiff Commonwealth Games.

There was no formal training for these Games, but the women's winter preparation kept their after-work and weekend hours very well occupied. Neither the Australian Olympic Federation nor the Australian Commonwealth Games Association had the funds to pay for athletes' travel expenses, and the government did not invest in sport as it does today. So fundraising was part of the preparation. Half-time race competitions during rugby league matches on suburban grounds—which Betty described as haphazard and unsatisfactory—were part of the fundraising effort for some of the athletes.

Some races were not so serious. Marlene and Betty, in club colours, fundraising during half-time at a rugby league match.

AUSTRALIAN CONSOLIDATED PRESS

GLORIA COOKE It would have been useful to have a little bit of psychology practised on us. It would have been nice to have someone say, 'C'mon, you can win. Do the best that you can'. We had George Saunders, who was a Melbourne masseur, but we didn't have too many people supporting us, in so far as doctors and psychologists. And certainly not dieticians … Each state had to raise money to send athletes overseas for an Olympic or Commonwealth Games. At the time, when Bob Menzies was Prime Minister, the government didn't provide enough funding to help the athletes get away. So our clubs had to get behind us. We used to walk around holding a blanket at half-time during first grade rugby league matches. We would hold out the blanket and spectators would throw in two bob [20 cents]. We raised a lot of the money ourselves.

Cardiff was Betty's first major overseas tour; thrilled anticipation, trepidation and tears marked the farewell to her family at the airport in Sydney. Betty would be away for two-and-a-half months, as she planned to travel in Europe after the Games with June Ferguson and some fellow athletes.

Before the Games opened, Betty and Ivan Lund, one of the team's fencers, were selected to represent the Australian athletes at a garden party at Buckingham Palace. Although the Queen was ill that day, and they also missed out on meeting Princess Margaret, just being there was an awe-inspiring experience for young Betty Cuthbert from Ermington.

The Athletes Village in Cardiff was part of a former Royal Air Force base and accommodation was basic: a dozen women to a hut, two per room. Despite the noisy environment, Betty felt as fit as she had ever been. She had been training hard—as usual—although without the constant strong competition that had prepared her so well for Melbourne. So she was stunned and disappointed when she struggled into fourth place in the 100 yards in 10.7 seconds. This time, Marlene Mathews won gold, with England's Heather Armitage-Young and Madeleine Weston running second and third. Marlene took gold again in the 220 yards, with Betty coming in second. The Australian relay team of Betty, Marlene, Kay Johnson and Wendy Hayes were easily beaten by the well drilled English team who set a new world record of 45.3 seconds ahead of Australia's 46.1 seconds.

Nevertheless, the journey was not over. During the short tour of Europe after the Cardiff Games, where Betty travelled with June Ferguson and a group of athletes including Herb Elliott, Norma Thrower and Dave Power, at June's instigation, Betty ran her first ever 400 metres in an international meeting in Goteborg (Gothenburg), Sweden—and won, in 54.4 seconds. In 1958, this win saw her ranked second in the world behind Maria Itkina of the Soviet Union. And Betty was also ranked second in the world in both the 100 yards and the 220 yards, behind Marlene.

There was other less formal competition too, during that brief European tour.

GLORIA COOKE   After the 1958 Commonwealth Games in Cardiff, some of the female athletes—Marlene, Betty, Norma Thrower, Michele Mason, Helen Frith, Bev Watson, Anna Pazera and myself—were invited to the Italian training camp, which was in the Italian Alps in a little town called Schio. Rome was coming up in two years, so it was considered to be good preparation.

I can remember us having lunch in this trattoria just before we competed. We thought the Italians were trying to sabotage us because they were serving spaghetti—trying to weigh us down. In those days, we thought spaghetti would be the worst thing in the world to eat. You had your steak and eggs before you competed. As it turns out, they were right and we were wrong. Pasta is one of the high-carbohydrate type foods that are recommended for athletes.

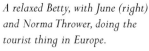

A relaxed Betty, with June (right) and Norma Thrower, doing the tourist thing in Europe.

AUSTRALIAN CONSOLIDATED PRESS

When Betty returned from Europe in October 1958, not even her mediocre performances in Cardiff could dampen the Australian public's enthusiasm: her local community still idolised their Golden Girl. A street procession formed part of the 'welcome home' celebrations, with Betty seated in state on a specially decorated float. When the procession stopped in the crowded main street of the new Ermington shopping centre, Betty was astonished to see that it had been named Cuthbert Avenue. (Later, the name was extended to Betty Cuthbert Avenue; it always gave her a thrill whenever she shopped there to think that this was her street.)

Once the excitement died down, Betty's lifestyle soon settled back into regular training, and running in interclub competitions. And, although she was still competing in the sprints, after that initial success in Sweden, she added 440 yards events to her repertoire. In January 1959, at a Saturday afternoon interclub meeting in only her fourth run over 440 yards, she ran 55.6 seconds to equal the world record.

Betty was in top form for the 1959–60 season. There were no national championships in 1959, but in the New South Wales state championships, she won the sprint double, beating Marlene in the 100 yards in 10.6 seconds and Robyn Scott in the 220 yards in 24.0 seconds. In the Trans-Tasman Cup, run in conjunction with the state titles, Betty also defeated New Zealand's Marise Chamberlain in the 440 yards in 54.3 seconds, smashing the world record by 1.3 seconds.

By the end of 1959, she had regained her number one ranking in the world for 100 yards (10.5 seconds) and 220 yards (23.5 seconds) and was still ranked equal second in the 440 yards. At the 1960 state championships, she again won the sprint double in fantastic times—wind assisted, so not valid for world records. Betty was in super form. On the third day of the championships, in an invitation 60 metres sprint, she broke the long-standing world record. The public adored her.

Betty poses under the sign for the newly renamed Cuthbert Avenue … or does she? This photograph is, in fact, recomposed from two separate images. A compositor at the newspaper which commissioned the photography stuck a photo of Betty on to a photo of the sign in order to place her in the best position to illustrate the story. AUSTRALIAN CONSOLIDATED PRESS

top and opposite: *Two angles on the same race. Betty wins a 100 yards interclub competition, with Marlene a close second and Gloria in third place, on the fast grass track of the Sydney Sports Ground.* L: BETTY CUTHBERT PERSONAL COLLECTION R: NATIONAL ARCHIVES OF AUSTRALIA

bottom left: *Betty, in her Cumberland uniform, demonstrates her distinctive style during an interclub race at the Sydney Sports Ground.* NEWSPIX

bottom right: *Betty practising her starts. Note the grass track.* NEWSPIX

DAVID PRINCE   Athletics received huge media exposure in the 1950s. During the summer period, from October through to March, every newspaper carried articles on interclub athletics in the same manner they would carry articles on cricket. Betty was big. She was breaking world records when running interclub events on the Sydney Sports Ground (which is now Aussie Stadium).

Every Saturday at 2 o'clock, the journalists would go to see the girls run on a very fast grass track at the Sydney Sports Ground. Then at 3 o'clock, they would cross the road to see the men's athletics at the old Moore Park cinders track.

Although a lot of Australian men's records were being broken weekly by the likes of Dave Power and Alby Thomas, they weren't likely to break world records. So the opportunity to see Betty Cuthbert and Marlene Mathews racing one another and breaking world records was viewed as one that shouldn't be missed.

Betty modelling the Australian team's uniforms for the Rome Olympics, accompanied by fellow team members: (left) Alby Thomas, at one stage a world mile record holder; (right and far right) Tony Madigan, Olympic boxer; (centre) John Konrads, fellow Olympic gold medallist in swimming. AAP/AP, BETTY CUTHBERT PERSONAL COLLECTION, NATIONAL ARCHIVES OF AUSTRALIA, AUSTRALIAN CONSOLIDATED PRESS

The 1960 Rome Olympics were not far off. At the main selection trials—the Australian national championships in Hobart—Betty was stung into action when she was easily beaten in the 100 yards by Queensland's Pat Duggan, 10.6 seconds to 10.9 seconds. Hitting back in the 220 yards, Betty set a new world record of 23.2 seconds and was once again selected for the Olympic sprint double and the relay. She was also appointed women's team captain. And training continued in earnest.

JUDY PATCHING We had special training sessions in the winter of 1960. We were in the southern hemisphere in Australia planning for Olympic competition in the northern hemisphere. So we had to try and compensate. We arranged for all members of the team to be billeted by someone in Sydney. We had good competition there and the athletes had their own coaches. Then we had a big meeting up in Newcastle where they had a record crowd of about 20,000 people.

So the preparation for Rome was excellent and it paid off for the distance runners, with Herb Elliott winning the gold medal in the 1500 metres and Dave Power getting a bronze in the 10,000 metres.

Betty was on track to retain her Olympic titles when tragedy struck in July 1960, only a few months before the Games. Running in a handicap race against men at half-time during a rugby league game at Henson Park, she tore a hamstring.

Although she was running again within three weeks, the injury had not healed properly. The long flight to Rome, followed by training on the hard European cinder tracks, aggravated it further. Betty managed to get through her heat of the 100 metres but, at the 90 metres mark in her quarter-final, she felt the leg go. Fourth place in 12.0 seconds saw her eliminated, and the injury prevented her from starting in the 200 metres and the relay. For Betty Cuthbert, just four years earlier Melbourne's Golden Girl, the Olympics were over. No doubt she cried tears of frustration at not being able to defend her Olympic titles. From her seat in the grandstand, Betty watched as the new wonder woman, Wilma Rudolph from Tennessee—the twentieth of her father's 22 children—took over her sprint titles.

Despite all this, by the end of 1960, she was still ranked number one in the world over 100 yards, and second in the world over 220 yards behind Olympic champion, Wilma Rudolph.

Betty's disappointment was tempered with relief, however. While her dedication to running was unquestionable, she did not live only to run. Quiet and unassuming, in some ways, she was glad of the opportunity to take a break from centre stage. And retirement after Rome had long been part of her plan.

DAVID PRINCE   I don't think Rome was as devastating to Betty as perhaps we think it should have been. If it was, she kept it to herself. Athletics to Betty wasn't the be-all and end-all of everything, unlike some other athletes whose whole life would centre on their particular sport. While she enjoyed so much success, it never affected her in the slightest. I think that's why she handled some of her disappointments pretty well, even though they were always kept on the inside.

opposite: *A proud Australian team marches at the Opening Ceremony of the Rome Olympics.*
NEWSPIX

But for the other members of the women's team, her injury was a major psychological blow.

JUDY PATCHING   Betty's lack of success due to her injury was devastating. I think we were more disappointed than Betty was. Here she was, this great performer in 1956, and four years later this happened. We all felt terribly upset and sorry for her. The disappointment in the track and field team was reflected in the rest of the women's performances. The only medal was a silver to Brenda Jones in the 800 metres.

In 1960, I went to Rome as the athletics manager and the whole aspect had changed since Melbourne. The partisanship was absolutely to the other extreme. The Europeans, and the Italians particularly, were strongly parochial. Wilma Rudolph of America won the women's 100 metres and 200 metres sprints, Germany's Armin Hary won the men's 100 metres and Italy's Livio Berruti won the 200 metres, so there was a spread of winners. But the partisanship was most noticeable. And the crowds weren't as great in the main stadium as they were at the MCG.

We faced tough competition from the American women in Rome. More American girls had come into athletics in those four years since Melbourne, so there was a very powerful American contingent. I think they all came from the one university. Add the fact that we were in Europe in their summer at the peak of their competition period. We were at a great disadvantage.

Certainly Wilma Rudolph was powerful. But that's not to say Betty would not have performed well if she had remained fit.

MARLENE MATHEWS   I retired after the Rome Games after having competed in national championships since 1950. I should have gone longer, as I always wanted to be the first woman to run 10 seconds flat for the 100 yards. But then I wanted to have a family also.

I don't have very many memories of the competition in Rome. The food wasn't what we were familiar with back at home. And I can remember the plumbing was terrible in the Village. We were told not to drink the water. I think most of us would drink Coke and eat chicken.

I was the only Australian who made the semi-finals of the women's 100 metres. But it was a bit of a disappointment not to make the final. I remember running in the heats at 9 o'clock in the morning. I got to about the 70 metres mark and it was like hitting a brick wall. We weren't used to running at that time of the morning. We had never come out and run heats of our events in the morning. Whereas now, if you have a heat at 6 o'clock in the morning, you would go out and train at 6 o'clock in the morning.

Another reason for the disappointing performances in Rome was that we didn't have the competition that we needed. We realised afterwards that we couldn't race only during our summer period and then have most of the winter off … If we were going to compete at international level, then it required a 12-month racing schedule.

Also, in 1956, we virtually had the women's sprints all to ourselves. The Europeans were still recovering from World War II. The Americans hadn't come into the sport to any great extent then. Of course, 1960 is notable for Wilma Rudolph's triumphs when she won the 100 metres and the 200 metres. By 1960, the rest of the world had started to catch up with us.

Despite the disappointing results overall, in other ways, the trip to Rome was a wonderful experience for Betty.

JUDY PATCHING The team split up after Rome and I took several athletes for a competition up in Oslo, Norway. After that we went down to the Welsh Games in Cardiff for a big athletic meeting, then back to London.

One evening in London, Kevan Gosper, Lloyd and Norma Fleming, the Skipper [Betty Cuthbert] and I fronted up to Talk Of The Town where Eartha Kitt was playing. We were wearing our team blazers, but the doorman said you couldn't get

in unless you wore a dinner suit with a bowtie. I said, 'You can tell the manager we've just been to Buckingham Palace to meet the Queen in these uniforms. Surely, we're good enough to come to this nightclub'.

Anyway, the manager invited us in, we had a top table and he put on champagne for us. I can't remember the Skipper having a drink. She liked to enjoy herself, although I would say she was always inclined to be fairly conservative.

They were the sorts of things we enjoyed behind the scenes. We had a wonderful time after Rome and it compensated for the terrible thing that happened to Betty with the hamstring injury. She enjoyed herself thoroughly. I think that alleviated her bitter disappointment to some degree.

GLORIA COOKE   I had some memorable experiences with Betty after the Rome Olympics. Some members of the athletics team went to London and competed with the British Commonwealth versus America. We also attended a big sports meet there that was sponsored by one of the newspapers.

Bet and I eventually came home by ship, which took five weeks. It was our second trip overseas to Europe, having been to Cardiff for the Commonwealth Games two years earlier. So like all young girls, we enjoyed seeing new things and going to new places. We went through the Suez Canal and stopped in Port Said, Aden, Colombo and Perth on the way home to Sydney. We would get off at the ports of call and buy souvenirs. We stored them in our cabin, much to the cabin boy's horror. It was just about full to the rafters. We bought dolls when we went to Naples. God knows why we bought them. I bought a camera. And we would buy hats and all sorts of funny things that took our fancy—nothing very expensive because we didn't have much money.

Coming home on the ship was an unforgettable experience and we had a great time together. Bet and I organised all of the sports on the ship. We made it really easy for the staff. In the end, they used to let us have the loud hailer to organise the deck sports, such as table tennis and quoits, and different things in the pool. Bet was great company.

As she had planned to do, after the Rome Olympics, Betty retired from athletics. She needed a break from training, running and the glare of the spotlight. For the next 14 months she thoroughly enjoyed herself, socialising with friends, working at the nursery and enjoying relaxed time with her family. She completely turned her back on athletics, refusing even to venture near a running track.

NORMA CROKER   Betty and I became friends through the Melbourne Olympics, when she was 18 and I was 22. Lloyd and I were married soon after the Games and Betty was still part of our life then. I gave birth to my daughter so I didn't go to the Commonwealth Games in Cardiff. But I got back into training and went to Rome. By that time, Betty and I had quite a strong friendship and she used to come up to stay at our place in Brisbane.

She was still very young and hated the publicity. She had a very strong will and that was obvious in the way she competed. But she was quite a shy person in her own way. For instance, if friends called in at our place, Betty would disappear because she thought they might have come to see her.

After a year or so of 'normal' life, however, Betty began to feel she was drifting aimlessly. Accustomed to the discipline of training and competing, she felt she needed something to focus on. She was working in the nursery one afternoon when the idea of making a comeback drifted into her mind. Her immediate instinct was to push the thought away, but it kept nagging at her, until she could no longer sleep properly. 'A voice was telling me that I had to run again', she told her friends, and later, the author Harry Gordon. 'I knew it was God and, even though I tried to resist, I finally just had to give in. It was quite clear.'

NORMA CROKER Betty had hinted that she wasn't 100 per cent fit prior to injuring her hamstring in Rome. I think she was bitterly disappointed but I don't think there were many tears. I think her concern then was to repair whatever was wrong. She was quite resigned to the fact that she was going to retire after Rome—she felt she had done all that God had asked her to do. But then she got this little voice that kept calling to tell her she had to run again.

After a 14-month absence from athletics, Betty resumed training in January 1962, setting her sights on selection for the 1962 Perth Commonwealth Games team. She trained through the summer and then spent time in Victoria training with Herb Elliott's likeable eccentric coach, Percy Cerutty, improving her endurance by running mile after mile through the tea-tree studded sandhills or along the golden beach.

HERB ELLIOTT When Betty decided to make her comeback she sought help from my old coach Percy Cerutty. They trained on the sandhills and beaches around Portsea on Victoria's Mornington Peninsula in preparation for the 1962 Commonwealth Games in Perth. Their relationship gelled because Percy understood that a coach must develop the mind, body and spirit of the athlete.

Preparation for training involved hammering starting blocks into the ground. Betty took a break from all this after Rome. NEWSPIX

I know that Percy had a great respect for Betty after her achievements in Melbourne. But he always held the view that women shouldn't be involved in the toughness of track and field. So there was potential for great conflict as Percy was a person of very strong views, which he expressed openly and without any diplomacy. Betty, of course, was a gold medallist, confident in her position as a female athlete … They brought their attitudes together and became very good friends.

I found Percy to be a genius. However, 50 per cent of what he said was genius and 50 per cent of what he said was rubbish. Betty and I both had the ability to select the 50 per cent that was helpful to us and not be deterred by the other 50 per cent. Some athletes weren't able to persist with him because of the contradiction of views—one day he would say one thing and another day he would say almost the opposite. Betty had the ability to sieve out those bits that weren't applicable to her and absorb those bits that were applicable and gain from them.

Percy had his affect on Betty, as he did on all of us who touched and understood his greatness. But Betty also had her affect on Percy—by changing his attitude to women athletes.

left and opposite: *Betty training in the sandhills at Portsea.*
L: THE HERALD & WEEKLY TIMES PHOTOGRAPHIC COLLECTION
R: AUSTRALIAN CONSOLIDATED PRESS

Once Betty began competing, her times improved rapidly. She won the 100 yards selection trial in 10.9 seconds on a rain-soaked track and came second in the 220 yards behind Joyce Bennett. In Perth, she was selected for the sprint double and the relay but for whatever reason, her times in the sprints were disappointing. No doubt the rain and the weather in general had something to do with it, as Perth during those Commonwealth Games was extremely hot. When the notorious cooling blast of the 'Fremantle Doctor' blew through, it created headwinds that slowed down all the sprint times. Betty finished fifth in the 100 yards semi-final in 11.0 seconds and was eliminated. And while she made it into the 220 yards final, she again finished fifth.

Disappointed in her performance, Betty asked Maisie McQuiston, the team manager, to withdraw her from the relay but fortunately, Maisie refused. She believed Betty was running well—and she was right. The Australians were trailing England by five yards when Betty took the baton for the final leg. It was just the challenge she needed. Emotionally revived and with mouth open wide, it was the Betty of old who caught England's Betty Moore and, with one last desperate 'kick', crossed the line first to win for Australia in 46.6 seconds. The crowd went wild, just as it had in Melbourne six years earlier.

In the final wash-up, overall results showed that, even after the hamstring injury, a long break and a limited competitive season, in 1962 Betty Cuthbert still ranked equal second in the world in the 100 yards with Robyn Scott and Britain's Commonwealth champion, Dorothy Hyman; and equal seventh over 220 yards.

The next major goal now for Betty and June was the 1964 Tokyo Olympics. Very early in 1963, June told Betty she would be running regular 440 yards events as well as the 100 and 200 metres sprints, and in February, Betty won the sprint treble at the New South Wales state championships. Over the next few months, she raced against Australia's best, winning the 100 yards and the 440 yards at the Moomba Carnival in

Melbourne, and the 440 yards in the national championships in Brisbane a couple of weeks later. Her other results in the nationals were respectable too: third in the 100 yards, and second in the 220 yards and the relay. Both women felt a trend was emerging and, on June's advice, Betty decided to concentrate on the 400 metres and focused her training on the longer distance.

TONY CHARLTON   At the Perth Commonwealth Games, Betty ran an inspirational final leg to help Australia to a gold medal in the 4x110 yards relay. However, she didn't make the final of the 100 yards after finishing fifth in her semi-final. And she was fifth in the final of the 220 yards. So people were writing her off, saying the glory years had come to an end. It was in that environment that her coach June Ferguson suggested she should think about running the 400 metres.

After her impressive start to 1963, and still ranking second in the world for the 100 yards and 440 yards, in October, Betty suffered an ankle injury and missed a month of proper training. Then, just after returning to competition, she suffered the foot injury that came close to putting an end to the second phase of her running career.

MIKE AGOSTINI Betty injured her instep before the Tokyo Olympics, which prevented her from competing and severely impaired her training. She thinks it may have happened while water-skiing on Narrabeen Lakes. One of the metatarsal bones in her foot had slipped out of place. I couldn't tell you how many doctors she went to. They couldn't give her any relief. Fortunately, she found John Nolan, and he was able to fix it.

Sports medicine was terrible then. There was no such thing as sports medicine per se. So Betty confided in me when she was looking for help. I dabble in various fields and learned to do manipulations, chiropractic treatments and all sorts of stuff.

But I was also a journalist and so I had to keep her secret. Betty wouldn't have gone to Tokyo if I had written the story for the *Daily Telegraph*. If an athlete had an injury in those days, more than likely, the Australian Olympic Committee or the Australian Athletics Association would have the person removed from the team.

So I kept my mouth shut about her injury and the story didn't come out until more than 10 years later. The inscription that Betty wrote for me in her autobiography says, 'Thanks for keeping my secret'.

The foot injury forced Betty to miss most of the 1963–64 interclub season and she just made the New South Wales team for the 1964 national championships in Melbourne. Although she was still training twice a day, the foot was very painful after each session.

It was all the more astonishing then that Betty managed to finish second at the national championships in Melbourne in the 440 yards behind Dixie Willis, and again behind Judy Amoore at the Moomba meet in Melbourne a week later. Invited to run in the WD & HO Wills fundraising carnival in Melbourne, while still battling the painful foot, Betty won the 400 metres in 53.5 seconds, easily beating Judy Amoore and Dixie Willis to ensure her place in the Tokyo Olympic team.

JUDY AMOORE   Betty was my idol when I was starting to run even though there wasn't much difference in age, with Betty two years older. She was a competitor and lived in Sydney, while I was in Melbourne.

I was very much the underdog for Tokyo as far as the selectors were concerned. I had just started running 400 metres, whereas Betty had established herself as the Golden Girl and Dixie Willis was the world record holder for 800 metres. The women's teams were very small in those days. And the selectors would not hesitate to trim them if they could. So it was assumed that not all three of us would be selected to compete in the 400 metres.

In 1964, we had three major 400 metres races in Melbourne: Dixie won the national championship, with Betty second. I won the Moomba meet at Olympic Park. Then, Betty was invited to run in the WD & HO Wills fundraising carnival at Olympic Park, where she easily beat Dixie and myself. So Betty, Dixie and I each won one of the races.

People in other track and field events should have been selected before me. Fortunately, my victory against Betty and Dixie in the lead-up race clinched my spot in the team. Dixie was chosen to run the 800 metres instead, although she didn't run in Tokyo.

I was very pleased to be selected, as it was my first international meet. My expectations were to run with grit and determination and hopefully a pleasing result would eventuate.

Clearly, the women were on friendly terms with each other. But by 1964, there had been unrest and conflict between administrators, trainers and competitors for some time.

RON CLARKE Before we went to Tokyo, the athletics team had a camp at Narrabeen on Sydney's northern beaches. Betty came along initially and then went off, saying it wasn't good enough for her. She was in her hometown and wanted to sleep in her own bed, train at her own facility and with her own coach. Then we had a manager threatening that he wouldn't allow her to compete in Tokyo. Dixie Willis also stormed off and there was real friction within the ladies' team.

I was aware of Betty's foot injury. You could have been thrown off the team if you were found to have an injury. That's one of the reasons why I wanted her away from the camp. I also didn't want the three managers interfering with her preparation.

As captain of the men's track and field team, I remember persuading Arthur Hodsdon and Ron Aitken to have a word with the managers and get them off Betty's back because she was liable not to go. They had already destabilised Dixie, who was a certainty to win the women's 800 metres before she went to Tokyo. I asked Ron to tell them to keep away from Betty Cuthbert: 'Let her train wherever she wants and with whom she wants. Whatever you do, don't try and threaten her'.

Betty's injury was now so bad, however, that she could no longer train. Once again, her career appeared to be in doubt until, in May 1964, she finally found a therapist who seemed to exercise a sixth sense in diagnosing and healing the injured foot.

TONY CHARLTON Betty had a very dubious preparation for the Tokyo Olympics because of that foot injury, which caused her great pain. It led to a conflict with the athletics administration of the time. And you can understand their point of view:

Betty's training prior to Tokyo was—as always—rigorous. Here, she practises her starts.

Betty wasn't running at interclub meets, nor was she running in state events. She couldn't. She was hobbling around and trying to keep the evidence of this injury from everybody.

Finally, after consulting various orthopods, chiropractors and physiotherapists, she was cured by a fellow in Sydney, John Nolan. Much later Betty told me the story in an interview that I did with her on television. Apparently, Nolan didn't even want to look at the X-rays of her foot. He said to Betty that she had a bone out of place. He then clicked it back in and she was able to resume proper training, but only after she had been to hell and back.

During the cold middle months of 1964, special winter competitions were held on Sundays, but persuading athletes to compete was a problem as they were in winter training. Fortunately for Betty, fellow 400 metres runners Jackie Byrnes (later Melinda Gainsford-Taylor's coach) and Bob Penfold were prepared to race her, providing the much-needed challenges that allowed her to stretch out and to sharpen her competitive edge. And in a further boost to her confidence, Betty had two good runs just prior to Tokyo, clocking 53.5 seconds in Newcastle and 53.9 seconds in Sydney.

JUDY PATCHING   I had a lot to do with Betty when she developed the trouble underneath her foot prior to the 1964 Olympics. People in the press had written her off. It didn't make sense to the press that this girl could go on and win the gold medal in Tokyo. But they had another think coming. Mount Everest was only a small peak to Betty Cuthbert.

By the time Betty arrived in Tokyo to compete in the 1964 Olympics, she was back in good shape and running well. Her biggest dangers for the Olympic title in the inaugural women's 400 metres were former world record holder Maria Itkina (USSR) and Ann Packer (Great Britain). The new world record holder, Sin Kim Dan from North Korea, was not running as she had competed in an unsanctioned meet a year earlier in Indonesia and was banned.

The Australian team's uniform was decidedly 60s at the Opening Ceremony for the Tokyo Games. NEWSPIX

Once again, Betty modelled for the team. BETTY CUTHBERT PERSONAL COLLECTION

Around the Village within the Australian team, a quiet buzz began to circulate. Could Betty Cuthbert possibly win a fourth gold medal? Surely not. She had not performed well in Rome. She had struggled with injuries. She was eight years older. The expectation seemed extreme: seemed like asking the impossible of her.

Her lead-up performances were reasonable, but not impressive. She qualified in third place in her heat, and ran second in her semi-final, well behind Ann Packer. So far so good, but still not an obvious winner. There was even debate in certain quarters about whether women should be running 400 metres at all.

JUDY AMOORE Percy Cerutty espoused in Tokyo that females should not be running 400 metres. As he often did, Percy shot off his mouth wherever he was. He thought 400 metres was too far and not a feminine thing to do. He said we were masculine and would be developing muscles on muscles …

My coach, Henri Schubert, happened to be travelling on the bus and took offence at Percy's comments. So he let him have it. Henri said, 'That's not true. Judy and Betty are both capable of running 400 metres. They're very feminine athletes and you shouldn't be saying things like that about them'.

Before the runners went out for the final, Betty was lying on a bench in the assembly area when an official said, 'It's time to go'. Her memory of that moment remains vivid: 'Something picked me up off the bench and did the rest for me'. And it does indeed seem that some mystical force must have been on her side. She drew lane two, the lane she wanted, with Judy Amoore in lane three, Maria Itkina in lane five and Ann Packer in lane six—all her strongest opposition strung across the track in front of her.

In front of 72,000 spectators at Tokyo's Olympic Stadium, Betty got off to an explosive start, then used the strong wind down the back straight to overtake Judy entering the final bend. She caught British champion Ann Packer just as they turned into the straight and led into the home turn two metres in front.

Her own words capture the intense struggle from there on: 'The wind was terrible and was like an invisible hand pushing against me. I was awfully tired then, but forced myself to keep driving ahead. I didn't think it would ever come to an end. My legs were getting heavier as the line edged closer. I wondered how Ann was going and if she had the strength to catch me. By then I knew either Ann or myself was going to win. I felt her right on my heels and knew she must have been just as tired as I was. But I wasn't going to be the first to give in and kept ploughing ahead for all I was worth. "Keep going", I said to myself. "Hold her off".'

She did exactly that, in what she later described as being 'the only perfect race I ever ran'.

In a thrilling comeback, Betty Cuthbert had won her fourth Olympic gold medal. Her time for the 400 metres was 52.0 seconds, 0.2 seconds clear of Ann Packer. Judy Amoore came in third to take the bronze.

right: *Going out in fine style: Betty displays her gold medal in Tokyo.*

opposite: *Running into history, Tokyo, 1964: Betty holds off Great Britain's Ann Packer to win gold in the 400 metres, while an exhausted Judy Amoore clinches the bronze for Australia.*
AAP/AP

ANN PACKER (in *The Pursuit of Sporting Excellence* by David Hemery) When I spoke to Betty years afterwards, I realised that I wouldn't know if I could ever have won that race. She is a mystical girl with very strong religious beliefs. I call her mystical because she has an inner understanding of herself, which would be very difficult for anyone else to touch. And I just felt that she had a stronger belief in herself than I had in myself. She has a very strong character and had many, many setbacks that motivated her tremendously. Her depth of reserve enabled her to keep coming back. That sort of spirit would be hard to beat.

JUDY PATCHING In the eyes of most people, Betty had achieved the impossible. It was an extraordinary victory and lifted the team tremendously. It was awe-inspiring. It was an amazing achievement when you analyse the setbacks she had and how she rose above it all ...

Packer went on to win the 800 metres gold medal.

And for Betty Cuthbert, Melbourne's Golden Girl, after 13 years of competitive running, it was all over. She never ran again. Later, speaking of her Tokyo win to author Harry Gordon, Betty recalled: 'It wasn't really me running. It was as if my body had been taken over. And I felt at great peace afterwards. I asked God, "Have I done enough?"'

It was indeed an extraordinary event, and for many of those who participated, or watched from the stands, the media box or on television at home in Australia, there are abiding memories.

JUDY AMOORE In the final, Ann Packer was drawn in lane six even though she was the fastest qualifier. In those days, the officials drew names out of a hat. They didn't give the best lane, for instance lane four, to the fastest qualifier. Betty drew lane two and I was in lane three. It was a standing joke between us that I always got the outside lane. I said she paid the officials or stacked the draw.

That was good for Bet because she knew I was a fast starter, so she could gauge her race by watching me when I was outside. I didn't think about it as much as Betty did.

opposite: A congratulatory touch from Ann Packer, as Betty and Judy share a hug. AAP/AP

above: *Judy and Betty pose with their medals during family celebrations.* JUDY POLLOCK PERSONAL COLLECTION

left: *Olympic medallists toast their success, 60s style.* JUDY POLLOCK PERSONAL COLLECTION

But I know she smiled inwardly and thought, 'Judy's out there, I've got to catch her first. And then I'll go for whoever else there is'.

It was a quick start because we had the wind behind us. We coasted down the back straight and Betty came up on me with about 180 metres to run. I remember thinking, 'We're both running well at the moment', and passing other competitors. But Ann Packer was well in front because of the staggered start.

We rounded the bend into the home straight and hit a headwind that nearly knocked us over. Betty went away from me and set out to catch Ann. I was thinking, 'I've just got to hang on'. I knew that I was in a shot for a medal if I stayed where I was. I fought that wind and managed to put one foot in front of the other.

I didn't know if Betty had won because I was so busy trying to keep myself on my feet. I remember walking over and giving her a hug. I said, 'Did you win?' And she nodded.

I also remember Bet lifting her arms up to the sky and I thought, 'You're saying a prayer'. And she was.

I wasn't expected to do anything in Tokyo. I had scraped into the team by the skin of my teeth. So I was overly delighted with the bronze medal. That was the start of my career. I came home thinking, 'I can beat anybody', whereas Betty had told me it was her last race.

Afterwards Betty and I had a special celebration aboard the *Fairsky*. Both our sets of parents were on the cruise ship in Yokohama. Judy Patching arranged our transport from the Village to meet them. The chefs made a cake with icing in the shape of a kangaroo and the Olympic rings and we all drank toasts to Betty and me. I've got a photograph of us sitting in front of the cake and we're both holding a champagne glass. But I don't think it went anywhere near our lips. We probably drank orange juice that night.

TONY CHARLTON Television coverage of the Olympic Games in 1964 was far removed from what it is in the 21st century. The most obvious difference is that the broadcast from Tokyo was black and white. From a commentary perspective, we

Sunday

Telegraph

Vol. XXV.   No. 49   Registered at the G.P.O. Sydney for transmission by post as a newspaper.   SYDNEY, SUNDAY, OCTOBER 18, 1964   N.S.W. PRICE 6d. (TASMANIA, WEST AUST. 1/-, OTHER STATES 9d)

WHAT A WEEK THIS WAS!

- **Labor's shaky hold in Britain** —Page 3
- **Morals arrest of President's aide** —Page 11
- **Kruschev—"schemer and braggart"** —Page 2
- *And at home* **YANGTZE WINS CUP** • *Back page*

DID CHINA BOMB MR. K?

Mao angry at double-cross

WASHINGTON, Sat. — Was Nikita Kruschev the first victim of Red China's nuclear bomb?

Western diplomats believe the Russian Premier was toppled from supreme power because he mishandled the Sino-Soviet row.

Kruschev's back-down on a promise to supply a sample atom bomb infuriated the Red Chinese leader Mao Tse-tung and probably was the main factor in cracking the Moscow-Peking axis.

Red China has alleged that Kruschev promised to give Peking nuclear know-how and the atom bomb, but in 1958 he renounced the agreement, withdrew his experts and recalled his scientists.

Behind the move was Kruschev's anxiety that nuclear power would make Red China too powerful. He did not believe apparently that Peking could go it alone.

Russian diplomats have, until recently, dismissed Peking's ability to produce a nuclear bomb.

Those who ousted Kruschev from the Kremlin apparently felt he mishandled the Sino-Soviet relationship and was therefore partly to blame for the rift with China and its disastrous consequences for the Communist bloc.

President Johnson yesterday described China's atom bomb as "an extremely crude weapon."

"But it means another nation can contaminate the atmosphere, and it means in due time, no doubt, they will have other weapons and develop the capacity to deliver them.

"It is really a sad day for the Chinese people because of all their hunger and misery. They have to take their resources and put them in nuclear weapons."

The American intelligence system had predicted Red China's nuclear blast.

On September 29, Secretary of State Dean Rusk announced to the world that China was then in a position to detonate its first nuclear device in the "near future."

Information

How the U.S. got its information on developments behind the Bamboo Curtain will remain a closely guarded secret.

The preparations may have been spotted by U-2 reconnaisance planes based on Formosa.

President Johnson said yesterday the U.S. by its own methods had confirmed that China had conducted a "low yield" atom bomb test in Western China.

U.S. experts said the explosion meant that China at this stage only had "associate membership" in the nuclear club and it would be probably a decade before she could qualify as full member with a complete system of nuclear weapons and aircraft or rockets to deliver them.

The experts said that intelligence from various sources suggested the device exploded was not a deliverable warhead or bomb and was probably built from the first sufficient amount of plutonium produced in China.

They said it would take from four to ten years to produce enough plutonium to build up a stockpile of 20 to 30 bombs and would take about the same time to develop the complex and expensive technology for making deliverable weapons.

China now has a small number of bombers, but they are old and of relatively short range. It would probably have to de-

Day that changed the world

—pages 7-11

● CONTINUED PAGE 2.

AND WHAT A GIRL SHE IS!

AUSTRALIA'S BETTY CUTHBERT flashes a radiant smile as she wears the gold medal she won at the Olympic Games in Tokyo yesterday.

BETTY WINS!

Betty Cuthbert yesterday won Australia's third gold medal of the Tokyo Olympics when she led all the way to win the final of the women's 400 metres.

Judy Amoore, Australia's other representative in the final, won a bronze medal by finishing third.

... and so does Bob!

Bob Windle last night won Australia's fourth gold medal when he won the 1500 metres freestyle.

Windle beat Nelson (U.S.A.), with Allan Wood (Australia) third and Russell Pegan (Australia) fifth.

Windle set an Olympic record — 17 minutes 17 seconds.

● FULL DETAILS SPORTS SECTION.

13 die in Indo. crash

DJAKARTA, Sat. — Thirteen passengers were killed on Friday when a Soviet-made Antonov-12 turboprop plane crashed and exploded in Palembang, Sumatra.

The military transport plane was carrying 60 Indonesian artists to "Crush Malaysia" rallies in the areas that border Malaysia.

The aircraft crash-landed because of faulty landing gear.

didn't know until the day before which events we were going to be covering. They were pooled services up until 1964. So the ABC and the commercial networks were all involved in the one coverage.

Since you didn't know which events you were going to be covering, you weren't able to sit down and study somebody's performance a year out. In that environment, I had very little preparation before calling the women's 400 metres final. Whereas others have been very complimentary about my call, I felt I could have done it much better.

Great Britain's Ann Packer firmed in favouritism after the first semi-final when she ran 52.7 seconds to street the field, which included Betty, who was second with a time of 53.8 seconds. Realistically, I didn't give Betty a chance of winning the final. With my heart, I hoped she could. But I thought Judy Amoore would pip her, given that she ran half a second quicker than Betty to win the second semi-final. Certainly, I thought Packer would beat Betty. Plus, there were other pretty good athletes in the field. The other finalists were Antonia Munkacsi of Hungary, Maria Itkina of Russia, M C van der Zwaard of Holland, Gertrud Schmidt of Germany and Evelyne Lebret of France.

But what happened? Our girl beat them all and won our only gold medal in track and field at that Tokyo Olympics. Betty's time of 52.0 seconds was 1.8 seconds faster than her performance in the semi-final. Packer was second in 52.2 seconds, which was a new European record, with Judy Amoore third in 53.4 seconds.

As I recall, Betty didn't start brilliantly but placed herself well down the back straight and ran the second turn well. Then, she really came home with a rush and outlasted Packer with an excellent run over the final 130 metres.

As Betty neared the finish line, I exclaimed, 'My God, she's going to win it'. It was such a huge upset and the words just came out of my mouth. But the station (which was the Nine Network) got quite a few complaints about that. Some people thought it was blasphemous.

Calling the inaugural women's final of the 400 metres at the 1964 Tokyo Olympics when Betty Cuthbert completed a miraculous comeback to win a fourth gold medal was one of the highlights of my Olympic broadcasting career.

opposite: *Betty makes front-page news once again.* AUSTRALIAN CONSOLIDATED PRESS

Betty's performance in Tokyo was marvellous because the odds were against it. How often do champions successfully make a comeback? After retirement, very few make it back.

Not only did Betty make a stunning comeback, many will agree with Tony Charlton that what she achieved in Tokyo remains one of Australia's all-time Olympic highlights.

BRUCE McAVANEY I think what stands out in the 400 metres final in Tokyo was Betty's courage. Betty had suffered a disrupted preparation due to injury and Great Britain's Ann Packer was an overwhelming favourite. And, as it was the first time the 400 metres had ever been run by women in the Olympics, Bet probably didn't know how to pace herself over the distance.

Betty's race in Tokyo wasn't a calculated run. There was a rawness, a naivety that was charming. She ran on instinct and pure ability and probably not a lot else, except a whole heap of courage. She was probably running on fear as much as anything else ...

The comparison that must be made is with Cathy Freeman, who ran two superb Olympic finals over 400 metres. Cathy was at the peak of her powers in 2000 at the Sydney Olympics. She was in better shape than in 1996 and had built a formidable reputation upon a long unbeaten stretch. She carried the same weight of favouritism as Marie-José Pérec of France, but 10 times the amount of pressure. No other athlete in my broadcasting career of 30 years has endured as much scrutiny as Cathy was under in 2000.

Knowing the disappointment if she didn't win, Cathy was able to implement a game plan. She was calculating, attacked from 200 metres and still had more in reserve if needed. She executed the race quite brilliantly ...

But Cathy's career was defined by one race. In 2000 it was either first or nothing. For Betty, her career revolved around four races.

Tokyo set her apart. Betty used her speed and had the courage to go out and take her chance. Here she was, eight years after her stunning debut on the world stage, against all the odds, stretched out in the 400 metres and winning her fourth Olympic gold medal. It's one of the great stories in sport.

One of the great stories indeed. And Betty herself claims that she was driven by a higher force; that God was on her side.

JUDY PATCHING She said she got this ethereal message from God that she was going to run and win the 400 metres in Tokyo. It's mystery book stuff.

MIKE AGOSTINI She had a precognition——foreknowledge through some meta-physical, spiritual sense——that she had won the race beforehand. As she entered the tunnel of the main stadium, Betty went into this time warp and knew that all she had to do was run. It wouldn't be easy, but she would win the race. It wasn't a dream. It wasn't a wish. It was a precognition.

HERB ELLIOTT One of the great things about sport is that it allows you to push beyond the boundaries to self-mastery and spirituality. Betty was always aware of the inner person——the body was just a vessel to carry around that inner spiritual being.

Whatever it was that spurred her on, the indisputable reality is that with her win in Tokyo, Betty earned a lasting place in the hearts and sporting history of Australia.

IAN HEADS In 1964 when Betty went to Tokyo, defied the odds and won the 400 metres gold, the cheering, love and goodwill for her from back home was just as powerful as it had been when she first stepped forward as our Golden Girl. That eight-year span of achievement in the most universal of all sports——running—— presents a powerful case for her having been, and being, our greatest of all Olympians. No other man or woman has won gold medals on the track at 100 metres, 200 metres and 400 metres.

I think the 1964 gold medal was the pinnacle of Betty's achievements because it was a triumph against the odds. It was just a gigantic moment.

TONY CHARLTON

All the hallmarks of a champion

'*A rare person who holds a rare place in Australian sport.*'

When Betty returned home from Tokyo, it was clear that this time, her retirement was official. Nevertheless, it took a while for her life to settle down into a 'normal' rhythm. As the nation's Golden Girl, and Our Betty—who had come blazing out of the shadows to claim that fourth gold medal—she was a model of determination, modesty, sweetness and sporting success that the public and the media was reluctant to let go of. Her score sheet recorded four Olympic gold medals, one gold and two silver Commonwealth Games medals, 16 world records, and numerous wins at national and state levels in Australia.

The many honours awarded her included the Helms Award (later called the World Trophy, from the Helms Athletic Foundation in the USA), the Sportsmen's Association of Australia's Walter Lindrum Award, and recognition in the 1965 Queen's Birthday Honours list.

At this stage in her life, Betty was ready to move on and expand her horizons. While still working occasionally in her father's nursery, she dabbled with coaching and studied massage and other alternative therapies, which had long held a fascination for her. She also pursued her interest in art and painting.

NORMA CROKER She was into alternative medicine years ago: the Bach flower remedies. She used to have these little bottles that would fix a cold. She had faith in it and it probably worked.

There was a sense that she was looking for a new purpose; something to focus on now that her athletics career was over. According to those who know her well, Betty was not interested in capitalising on her former glory, remaining surprisingly unaffected by her achievements and the national standing they had earned her.

GLORIA COOKE Over the years I've known her, Betty never changed very much, even after the 1956 Olympics. Success didn't go to her head in any way. She was always a very down-to-earth person and quiet. She was always very modest.

Very modest, and very unassuming. These qualities pervaded all areas of Betty's life, including the romantic. As attractive as she was, and as well known and highly regarded, a long-term relationship and marriage were not to be, although old

134

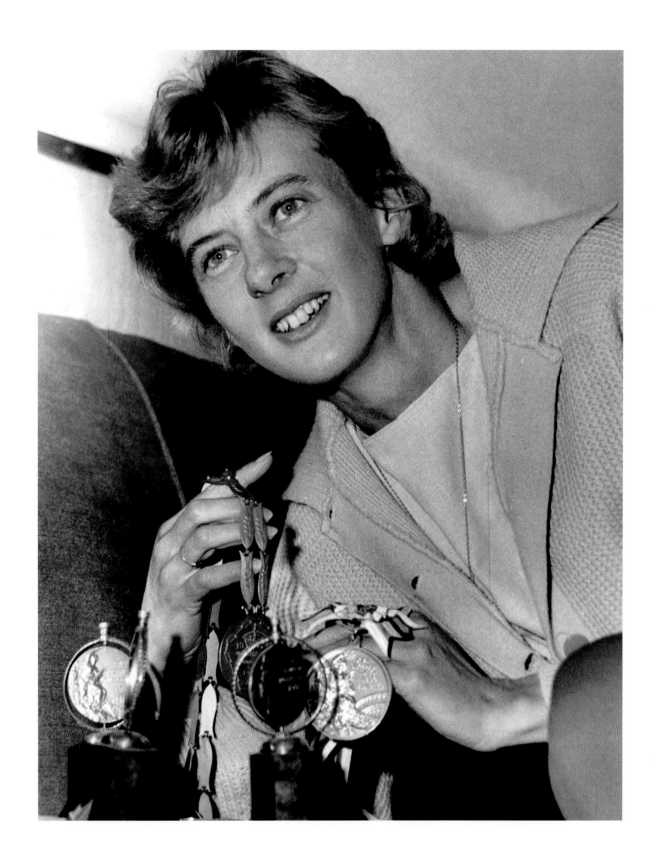

friends believe Betty would have been happy to settle down to family life once she had stopped running.

JUDY PATCHING Inside of her she wanted to meet a nice bloke. But she had this extraordinary attitude: she felt men weren't interested in her as a girl; they were interested in her as an athlete. That barrier was one of the reasons she never finished up with a guy and got married, which was a bloody shame.

left: *A privileged group of women at one of Betty's fitness classes.*
NEWSPIX

opposite: *Betty appeared alongside other international athletes in Adidas promotions.*
NEWSPIX

In any case, Betty was making the most of her skills and training. She was quietly exploring new avenues and enjoying life. By the late 1960s, she was conducting ladies' fitness classes and beginning to build a career in the area of health and fitness. It was at this time, around October 1969, that she first noticed the strange, subtle symptoms that—although it took many years to confirm the diagnosis— heralded the onset of multiple sclerosis (MS).

Betty recalls: 'I began to notice tingling in my hands, similar to the familiar pins- and-needles sensation when a limb "falls asleep". If I walked any distance, similar sensations appeared in my legs and feet. Sometimes, when my clothes brushed against me, I'd tingle all over. It was very strange …'

Over the next few weeks, the symptoms gradually worsened. The right side of her face became numb, so that she would bite her tongue without realising. Never a clumsy person, now she found herself dropping plates and bowls. Her coordination started to play up, and it became a real task for her to pick up small objects. Her left leg began to throw out involuntarily while she was walking. Desperately worried by now, Betty tried to hide her symptoms and did not confide in anyone.

By mid December 1969, however, when the symptoms became too intrusive for her to ignore, she finally sought specialist medical opinion. Between December 1969 and January 1970, she underwent various tests and treatments. The testing process, which included a 24-hour stay in hospital, did not produce conclusive results—a scenario typical of MS diagnosis in those days. The treatment incorporated a course of eight vitamin B12 injections.

Feeling much better, and with no clear diagnosis, Betty decided to get on with her life. Her old friend and training mate, David Prince, was looking for 'star' staff to work with him promoting Adidas sports products. When he offered Betty a job, she was happy to accept.

DAVID PRINCE I was responsible for employing Betty in the 1970s after I left school teaching to work in New South Wales as a state manager for a company that distributed Adidas. Ron Clarke was in the head office and my role was to get some sports stars on the staff. In one year, our sales team included Betty, the swimmer Shane Gould, the great North Sydney rugby league winger Kenny Irvine and the number one soccer referee in Australia, Tony Boscovich. It was like a who's who of sport in Australia. Bet wasn't cut out for a sales person, but she was a great promotions and public relations lady.

For the next few years, everything seemed to be all right. Betty liked the challenges offered by her job, and spent time with friends new and old. Her sweet nature, compassion and generosity ensured her popularity at work and socially, and she made a point of keeping in contact with many of her friends from the hard-training, heady athletics years.

JUDY AMOORE I didn't really get to know Betty as a personal friend until Tokyo and then after. Betty was a great help to me when I got injured before the 1972 Olympics in Munich. I had a calf muscle tear and wasn't going to be selected in the team. I had been trying to hide my injury from everybody. If you told anyone you were injured, the selectors could drop you straight away. I had lots of treatment before the doctor put me in a plaster cast and said: 'You can't go'. Of course, it was all over the media by that stage.

Then Bet rang me from Sydney and said, 'Come up here. I can help you'. So that was all I needed. My husband looked after our two children and I flew up to Sydney and stayed with Bet and her parents at their home in Ermington. Every day, she took me to a masseur that she had used. He treated me and I kept training. Betty looked after me like a lost child.

I was required to prove my fitness with a time trial in Sydney, which I ran well inside the selectors' expectations. So I did get on the plane and went to Munich as captain of the women's track and field team. Without Betty, I would never have got there.

Unfortunately, I didn't run in the finish. I completely ripped my calf muscle during a training run just two days before I was due to compete ... Bet was very sad about that and so was I. But she certainly got me through a very difficult period.

Doing well in her new career, Betty decided to move out into a home of her own. Life was good: busy, happy, fulfilling. But as 1973 wore on, the worrying old symptoms reappeared. By early 1974, Betty knew she had a serious problem. This time, she was determined to get a definitive diagnosis. The neurologist she saw in February 1974 ran further tests, and now there was no doubt: MS—no known cure, gradual progressive degeneration; rate of progression highly variable from patient to patient. The specialist advised Betty not to tell her employers, since

Post-athletics, Betty had time to pursue other passions.
THE HERALD & WEEKLY TIMES
PHOTOGRAPHIC COLLECTION

138

many MS sufferers were able to continue normal life and work for many years, even if at a slightly reduced pace at times. So Betty kept the diagnosis close to her chest, telling only her mother and her close friend, Mike Agostini.

She continued to build her career in sporting goods, opening a New South Wales branch office for the newly established sports clothing company, Le Coq Sportif, in the mid 1970s. She was also the astonished subject of the popular national television show, *This Is Your Life*; at that stage, none of the friends and family who appeared on the show was aware of her illness.

A short time later, in an exciting new venture, Betty went into partnership in a suburban sports shop with her old friend, Bill Westerveld, who had supplied her first pair of running shoes in 1960 when he was an Adidas rep.

Marion Cuthbert, Betty and a youthful Mike Willesee, host of This Is Your Life, *pose with some of Betty's family and friends including Judy Amoore, standing behind Marion.* JUDY POLLOCK PERSONAL COLLECTION

But the demon followed. Her MS symptoms worsened.

Through that second half of the 1970s, as she slowly became increasingly debilitated, there were periods of despair when Betty sought and found comfort in the Christian church. She had always had faith in God and it was second nature for her to turn to Him for help and support, although then, she was not aligned with any particular denomination or church community.

She had reached a stage of debility where it was exhausting for her to comb her hair or brush her teeth. She needed constant rest periods when working in the shop. Controlling her right arm became a problem. 'Aiming for a light switch or a keyhole, I'd watch helplessly as my arm waved around in mid-air before reaching the spot I was aiming for', she says. 'Putting makeup on became increasingly difficult. My left hand had to support and steady my right as I gingerly applied lipstick and mascara.'

Socialising: Betty keeps company with legendary American athlete, Jesse Owens, and Australia's Dawn Fraser. NEWSPIX

Eventually, she could no longer run the shop nor fend for herself at her small house where she'd been living alone since 1971. Reluctantly, Betty moved in with her sister, Jean. Even then, despite the fact that there was obviously something terribly wrong, few knew the details of Betty's illness.

Desperate for healing now, Betty flew with a doctor friend to a clinic in Los Angeles, where for six weeks she was treated with a mixture of acupuncture, homeopathic injections, a natural food diet and ultrasonic massage. She returned home feeling much better and optimistic that the progress of the disease had been halted. In September 1979 she finally went public with her story, telling it through her old Olympic friend and journalist, Mike Agostini, in the *Australian Women's Weekly*.

MIKE AGOSTINI She told me about her MS long before it was announced and I didn't tell anyone. If you have a friend, you don't divulge their secrets. When doctor Ken Cooper, the aerobics guru, was out here in the late 1970s, Betty asked me whether she could consult him about it. So I arranged for her to talk to Ken.

By 1979, there were rumours everywhere about Betty's condition. We talked about it and when she was ready to make the announcement, I approached Ita Buttrose, who I have known since she was a teenager. The *Australian Women's Weekly* paid us a handsome sum for the exclusive and we shared equally. The article describes exactly how she discovered MS and how she was aware that something was wrong.

But the demon hadn't finished with her and there began a continuous and draining saga of hope and frustration, of effort and sorrow, and of uncontrollable emotions. While retaining a belief that a cure for MS might eventually be found, Betty turned increasingly to her strong Christian faith to sustain her as she lived 'one day at a time'.

Sometimes, her faith was stretched to the limit. At the age of 41, Australia's Golden Girl reluctantly applied for and was granted a government invalid pension. A year later, the Department of Social Security—having deemed that the interest from her bank savings was beyond the permitted limit—reduced the pension. Betty went to the press, which she was not prone to doing, and eventually her full pension was restored. But there was never an apology.

The Australian Women's Weekly *broke the story of Betty's condition in a lengthy article by her friend and fellow Olympian, Mike Agostini.*
AUSTRALIAN CONSOLIDATED PRESS

In the early 1980s, Betty began to feel restless living in Sydney and, after much thought, decided to move to the quietness and relative solitude of the countryside, into a little house about 20 kilometres north of Lismore, near Dunoon. She named the house 'Braeside', Scottish for 'Hill Slopes'.

It was a good move. Country life agreed with her and as the months went by she started to feel better than she had when living in the city. 'I felt my old zest for life returning', she says. Wonderful neighbours watched over her and she enjoyed living alone. Betty also began assisting the MS Society and was invited to join the Advertising Standards Council, which meant travelling to Sydney every month. It was a time of regeneration for her.

Given her strong Christian faith, it is not surprising that when the Reverend Gordon Moyes of Sydney's Wesley Mission visited Lismore in May, 1985, Betty attended his service in the town hall. Betty says that when Reverend Moyes invited people who wanted to become Christians to join him at the front of the hall, she went hot, then cold and started to tremble. Her heart thumped. She didn't know what it was about, but knew she had to go forward.

In the ceremony that followed, Betty was 'born again'. 'All of a sudden', she says, 'I had a new and unexpected sense of assurance that I belonged to God.' She says that the feeling was 'honestly better than winning four gold medals. To be born again is the best medal anyone can ever get, and you don't have to train for it!'

Even before that eventful day, Betty felt that her time at 'Braeside' was coming to an end. So when she was invited to the opening of the Pentecostal Rhema Family Church in Perth, she did not hesitate. She says she felt the same urge she had before leaving Sydney.

At Rhema she met up again with the champion tennis player Margaret Court, who was deeply involved with the church. Their paths had crossed many times before. Margaret invited her home. They talked at length.

To the considerable dismay of her family, Betty decided to move to Perth. She really had no friends or relatives in Western Australia, but she was determined to go. In September 1985, she packed up her home in Lismore, flew to Perth and moved into a rented flat in Nedlands.

For the next two years, she attended the Bible school associated with Rhema, where she says she learned to study the word of God, to meditate on it and digest it. It was exhausting but exhilarating. After finishing the course, she returned to normal life and towards the end of 1988, bought a place in Como: a downstairs unit on flat ground, with the ease of access she needed. As the MS slowly but steadily progressed, she began to use a wheelchair indoors, and an electric scooter to get around outdoors.

In early 1991, at a meeting of the new Margaret Court Ministries, Betty met Rhonda Gillam, a pleasant women about her own age. A short while later, Rhonda invited Betty to spend a weekend with herself and her husband Keith at their home in Mandurah, an hour's drive down the coast from Perth.

Thus began an enduring and inspiring relationship. By September that year, Betty had sold her place in Como and moved into a unit in Mandurah just around the corner from Rhonda and Keith's place. Rhonda, convinced that God has chosen her to look after Betty, has become Betty's carer, confidante, secretary, housekeeper, spokesperson, beautician, hairdresser, podiatrist, taxi driver and constant companion.

JUDY PATCHING   Rhonda Gillam is an absolutely wonderful woman. It's a God-given blessing that she's there looking after Betty.

In September 1993, Rhonda and Betty were driving home from Perth when they heard on the radio that Mandurah had been hit by powerful winds. They arrived to find that a 200 kph mini-tornado had torn through two units, one of them Betty's. 'Where my beautiful little unit had stood that morning, there was now a tangled mess of bricks and wood and smashed furniture and glass', recalls Betty. Most of the roof had fallen in. Her massage room was almost totally blown away. One bedroom was reasonably intact, so what could be found was stacked in there. Fortunately, almost all her memorabilia and important personal possessions were safe.

That same day, it was announced that Sydney had been awarded the 2000 Olympic Games.

Betty and Rhonda were still cleaning up in the aftermath of the tornado when they received an invitation to the Australian Sports Hall of Fame Champions Dinner in Melbourne, and decided they should attend. When the MC called Betty's name, she had no idea that she was to be inducted as a 'living legend', but as the spotlight fell upon her, 700 people rose and burst into applause. For the next 30 minutes, she sat there in tears as her career and achievements were highlighted. Her Mum and her sister Midge were there, along with June Ferguson, frail after suffering a stroke.

In ensuing years, Betty was also nominated for the 'World Sports Awards of the Century' and named one of Australia's 'Living National Treasures' by the National Trust. The first stadium built at Homebush for the Sydney Olympics was named after her, as was one of the Sydney harbour ferries.

In 1996, concerned that Betty might be struggling on her invalid pension, Betty's old friend John Singleton and sports promoter and manager Max Markson decided to help her out financially, raising $270,000 at a testimonial lunch in Sydney.

With the testimonial money, Betty bought a grassy two-hectare block east of Mandurah where she and Rhonda regularly enjoyed picnic lunches. They spoke of Betty's plans to build small units on the block so that underprivileged mums and their children could come for a break.

above: *John Singleton shares a happy moment with Betty.* BETTY CUTHBERT PERSONAL COLLECTION

left: *Betty launches the Sydney ferry named in her honour.* NEWSPIX

On one of those outings at the block they encountered a man who was searching out property in the area. They shared lunch and found him to be charming company, as well as a born again Christian. He explained that he had done time in gaol for a bank robbery, but had seen the error of his ways and converted to Christianity. He'd worked as an evangelist, he said, and at the time was involved in various kinds of business and charity work.

Betty became excited by his apparent sincerity and enthusiasm. He too wanted to help others and at subsequent meetings he proposed setting up a trust fund to raise money to finance the building on Betty's block. Over the ensuing months, Betty and Rhonda mortgaged the block and a unit Rhonda owned, trusting that their new-found friend and colleague was making wise investments on their behalves. By the time this conman disappeared, Betty and Rhonda had lost almost $400,000 between them, and had 'crippling mortgages on properties that we previously owned outright'.

They weren't the only ones. Others in Mandurah and interstate later revealed that they too had been victims of the same scammer. He was eventually convicted of fraud and gaoled in South Australia.

Rhonda and Betty scrambled together enough money to make the first of two mortgage repayments, but they didn't know how they could make another. Their misfortune became public. It was suggested that Betty sell her Olympic gold medals, but she adamantly refused.

People began stepping forward to help. One prominent sportsman asked how much they had lost then, for 15 months, made a monthly payment into their account to help repay their loans. As soon as it could be arranged, Rhonda put her unit on the market and Betty reluctantly did the same with her block.

Then in March 1999, a fundraising lunch was organised to help out.

RON CLARKE   Betty had some real financial problems in the late 1990s after she and her carer, Rhonda Gillam, were taken down by a conman in a failed business venture. Just before the Sydney Olympics, I helped to arrange a beneficiary dinner for her in Melbourne. As I was based on the Gold Coast, Dick Wicks and Peter Bartels from the Australian Sports Commission put in a huge effort to organise the dinner. We got a great reception from everybody. Peter asked the Prime Minister, John Howard, to attend. Cathy Freeman came along as well as a lot of Olympians from 1956. Betty couldn't make it, because she was so ill at that stage. But we got her and Rhonda on a direct line via television. We had great support from big business and raised a substantial sum, in excess of $150,000. It signified the affection that people have for Betty. She is held in awe because of the way she has quietly fought MS and got on with life. I think everyone admires the courage she has shown.

As a result of this fundraiser, the mortgage on Betty's block was completely paid off. And despite the ordeal, Betty maintained her faith in God and in human nature.

NORMA CROKER It should have knocked Betty around when she lost all the money to the conman. I think she and Rhonda were both gullible and this guy had done his homework very well. He knew exactly what point to hit on. And they handed over all this money. But she can accept that as God's will. She quite amazes me. She feels that because of her high profile, people will be made aware of unscrupulous people so it won't happen to them. She's quite a Pollyanna in lots of ways. Old Pollyanna could always justify things that went wrong.

By this stage, Australians were being swept along in the excitement of the rapidly approaching 2000 Sydney Olympics. The big question—and a brilliantly kept secret—was: 'Who will light the cauldron at the Opening Ceremony?' Names like Murray Rose, Herb Elliott, Marjorie Jackson, Dawn Fraser, Shirley Strickland and Betty Cuthbert were all mentioned and speculation was rife.

Betty was secretly advised that she would play a part in the Opening Ceremony; that she would be going around the arena with other Olympians, pushed in her wheelchair by Raelene Boyle. That was all she knew.

It wasn't until that spectacular night that Betty realised she and Raelene were the ones chosen to carry the flame into the arena in a celebration of 100 years of women's participation in the Olympic Games.

above: *Rhonda and Betty with Betty's good friend, former boss and Olympian, Ron Clarke.* BETTY CUTHBERT PERSONAL COLLECTION

opposite: *Sporting royalty: six of Australia's most famous Olympians from the track and pool: (clockwise from top left) Murray Rose, Marjorie Jackson, Herb Elliott, Shirley Strickland, Dawn Fraser and Betty Cuthbert. All were considered favourites to light the cauldron at the Opening Ceremony of the Sydney Olympics.* NEWSPIX

She recalls the moment. 'I've never heard anything like the tidal wave of sound that greeted us. It brought me alive. I think it nearly lifted me out of my chair! I looked around at the tens of thousands of torches waving in the stands and flashbulbs exploding from every direction. All I wanted to do was wave and wave in appreciation. As Raelene started to push me around the running track she leant over and said, "Wow!" There wasn't much else you could say. It was overwhelming.'

Then into the spotlight came the next 'runner': Dawn Fraser. With a kiss, Betty and Raelene passed the torch to her. Dawn carried it on to Shirley Strickland, who carried it to Shane Gould, who in turn carried it around to Debbie Flintoff-King. Running down the aisle that split the thousands of competitors, Debbie handed it to a glowing Cathy Freeman, who was waiting at the foot of the huge podium. Spellbound, the vast crowd watched as Cathy climbed the stairs, walked into the glistening pool of water and put the torch to the cauldron.

The Games of the XXVII Olympiad were under way.

Betty didn't attend many events in the first week, reserving her strength for the athletics program. Of course, Cathy Freeman's 400 metres gold medal was the highlight: the first track and field gold medal for Australia in a dozen years. It brought back so many wonderful memories for the watching Golden Girl.

And after all the years, memories of her achievements were still vibrant for many in the crowd. Everyone seemed to remember Betty: she was amazed and delighted at how many people wanted their photo taken alongside her.

But when the Games ended, Betty returned home to Mandurah; back to the rhythm of everyday life with her new cat, Emmi. The fan mail increased after her very public Olympic appearances, but not much else changed.

The MS was slowly progressing, and Betty's general health was deteriorating. In late September 2002, she was undergoing a day procedure for severe nerve pain in her face when she collapsed and was rushed to hospital suffering bleeding to the brain. Initially, she was admitted to Perth's Mount Hospital, but when her condition deteriorated she was transferred to Royal Perth Hospital.

top and below: *At the opening ceremony of the 2000 Sydney Olympics, Raelene Boyle (Australia's finest athlete to never win an Olympic gold medal) has the honour of entering the main stadium with Australia's most decorated athlete, Betty Cuthbert. They meet up with a group of this country's greatest sportswomen as a tribute to the role women have played in the Games.* T: AUSTRALIAN PICTURE LIBRARY B: JULIAN SMITH/AAP IMAGE

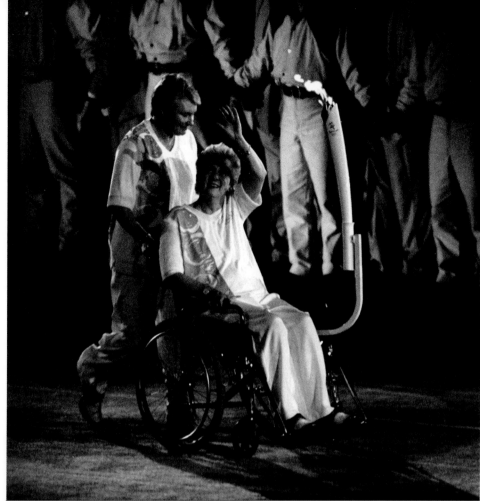

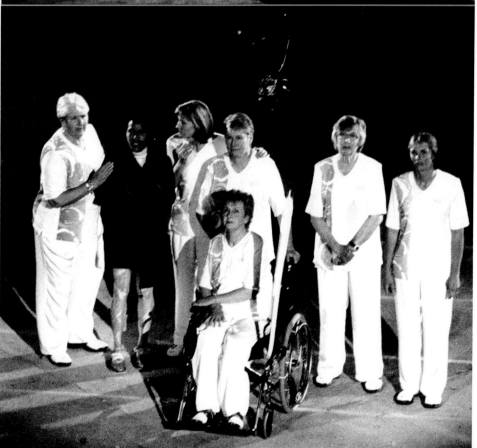

'She was admitted in a critical but stable condition but her condition has deteriorated further overnight', said a hospital spokeswoman. The prognosis for the Golden Girl was very, very poor. A saddened nation waited anxiously.

But Betty had already shown that she could fight harder and longer and more successfully than most. She had four pieces of gold to prove that, and although there was talk as she slowly recovered of her needing to enter a nursing home, she and her friends were adamant that would not happen. After three months in hospital, she returned to her own home.

Just over two years later, on 3 December 2004, her coach June Ferguson passed away, aged 76. When June retired in 1988, her athletes, including four Olympians, had achieved more than 200 NSW titles; more than 30 state records; more than 60 national wins and places; 16 world records; and five Olympic gold medals.

Her death meant that one of the world's greatest athletic partnerships was suddenly dissolved. No doubt June's last words to Betty would have been for the Golden Girl to keep fighting her considerable physical problems with everything she had; to stay in front of the opposition and never to give up.

In June 2005, Betty's Mum—who had provided so much support—also died.

Nowadays, Betty's long-term memory isn't especially good, although she always remembers her friend, Robbie Webster's birthday: 'How could I ever forget? That's the day I won my fourth Olympic gold medal'. She's confined full-time to her wheelchair, cannot move her feet or any part of her body, has to be turned in bed at night and can only use her left hand to clean her teeth and feed herself.

'She's almost totally disabled', says Rhonda, 'but because of her attitude and amazing faith, nobody believes this to be so. And people should know.

'I just feel privileged that God has chosen me to look after her.'

Rhonda and other church friends care for all Betty's daily needs. The Golden Girl regularly welcomes visitors to her Mandurah home, still travels occasionally to special events, and keeps all her remarkable memorabilia and photographs hanging on her unit walls as constant reminders. Most importantly, her spirit remains as buoyant as ever.

One of Betty's recent trips was to the Commonwealth Games in Melbourne where, Rhonda says, 'The crowds loved her … and something special happens to her too on such occasions. They love her because of her adorable, peaceful nature and quiet demeanour'.

So many people love Betty Cuthbert—for the person she is and the inspiration she provides.

IAN HEADS   Today, she is up there where she belongs—at the very top of the tree whenever the dual subjects of Australian sport and achievement are under discussion.

British Olympic champion Sebastian Coe and broadcaster Bruce McAvaney pose with Betty and Rhonda. BETTY CUTHBERT PERSONAL COLLECTION

BRUCE McAVANEY   Betty Cuthbert still has that unique spot in Olympic history. She is the only male or female to win the 100 metres, 200 metres and 400 metres at the Olympics. It's an unlikely treble …

It puts Betty on a pedestal on which she stands alone. I've always thought that she's, arguably, our greatest-ever Olympian. Dawn Fraser and Ian Thorpe would come into consideration, with four and five gold medals, respectively. Dawn had the unique achievement of winning the same event—the women's 100 metres freestyle—at three successive Olympics until Hungarian Krisztina Egerszegi equalled the feat with a third successive gold in the 200 metres backstroke. For Ian, another chapter may yet be written in Beijing.

However, I would lean towards Betty as our greatest-ever Olympian for what she achieved in 1956—because Melbourne was so important for us as a young nation—and then for what she was able to do eight years later in Tokyo.

Running Spike worn by
Betty Cuthbert, A.M., O.B.E.

Betty is a rare person who holds a rare place in Australian sport.

I'm very fond of Betty and I get a bit emotional when I think about her, to be honest. I think she's a wonderful lady. She's got the kindest heart and she's a beautiful spirit. She is good at just about everything she looks at. And she's been very sick and very brave. I think a lot of her. She is one of my all-time favourite people and athletes.

above and right: *Betty with good friend and fellow athlete, Herb Elliott.* BETTY CUTHBERT PERSONAL COLLECTION

opposite: *One of Betty's running shoes from her Tokyo win has been gold plated and preserved for posterity.* KEN MATTS/NEWS LTD

HERB ELLIOTT   Betty Cuthbert and Shirley Strickland would have to be the two best female athletes that Australia has ever produced. As far as I'm concerned, Betty is the greatest …

After the Empire Games in 1958, a whole group of us——Betty, myself and six other athletes——travelled in a Volkswagen van from London, across the channel, through Europe up to Stockholm for competition. I got to know Betty as a gentle person with an ever-ready friendly smile, unselfish, self-contained but at personal peace.

She is a person whose company I've always enjoyed. I admire her quiet strength. She's a person who gets on with the job and doesn't whinge and moan. She's able to turn a negative into a positive. Betty has all the hallmarks of a champion.

TONY CHARLTON It was never easy for Betty. Sure, she had all of these gifts, the physical attributes and the smile. But there were plenty of downers in between. And she had stiff opposition from the likes of Marlene Mathews, Norma Croker, Judy Amoore and Dixie Willis. Our girls were pretty good.

By any measure, she was the most remarkable athlete. She won three gold medals in one meet and then won a fourth in an improbable comeback. But I'm inclined to think that her greatest triumph—and greatest struggle—has been the health battle against multiple sclerosis.

My friendship with Betty has stretched for more than half a century. As a broadcaster, I found Betty to be delightful, retiring. She didn't push herself. I think one of her endearing features is her wistfulness. She has a winning smile and looked very attractive on the track, hence the Golden Girl. She had the crowd on her side. And she has always been possessed of a decency and first-rate character, otherwise she would never have gotten through. She is greatly loved. In today's era, with all of the endorsement opportunities, she would be a millionairess.

I continued my association with Betty when I was a councillor for The Royal Flying Doctor Service and chairman of the Alfred Hospital Foundation. Despite her disability, she kindly attended some of our charity events. I fondly remember pushing her around in a wheelchair. Those sorts of things cement a relationship.

On top of that, she sent me a copy of her autobiography, *The Golden Girl*. She penned a lovely note inside it, which said, 'From one who will never forget your words, "My God, she's going to win it"'. It meant a lot to me because it was from such a marvellous person whom I greatly admire.

NORMA CROKER In Betty's last book, she quotes all sorts of verses from the Bible. Her faith has kept her going. People ask her, 'Do you blame God for your illness?' No. Betty feels that her high profile allows her many battles with adversity to raise awareness in other people, so that they can relate to them better. It's an amazing faith.

JUDY AMOORE Betty has enormous faith. She always has done. And that's what is very special about her. She's been amazing with what she's been through with MS. She's so unassuming and yet so gracious with everyone and everything she encounters.

Judy Amoore and Betty reminisce at the Commonwealth Games in Melbourne, 2006. JUDY POLLOCK PERSONAL COLLECTION

We have lots of connections in those areas, such as the belief in our ability to run fast and face life's hurdles throughout our journey.

Betty is always willing to share her life experiences with me and I feel very privileged to be part of her life. I'm honoured that our love and respect for each other enables her to make me a lifelong friend and confidante.

JUDY PATCHING   She's an extraordinary girl, ultra sincere and too trusting. I've never heard her complain. Ever. She's got some great in-built iron fortitude, which the ordinary person hasn't got. On top of that, now she's got infinite faith. When you put these two things together, you're up against powerful elements.

below left: *Clockwise from top left: Raelene Boyle, Judy Patching, Laurie Lawrence, Dawn Fraser, Betty and Marjorie Jackson-Nelson.* THE HERALD & WEEKLY TIMES PHOTOGRAPHIC COLLECTION

below right: *Betty with former IOC president Juan Antonio Samaranch, Judy Patching, and Bill Berge Phillips, President of FINA.* BETTY CUTHBERT PERSONAL COLLECTION

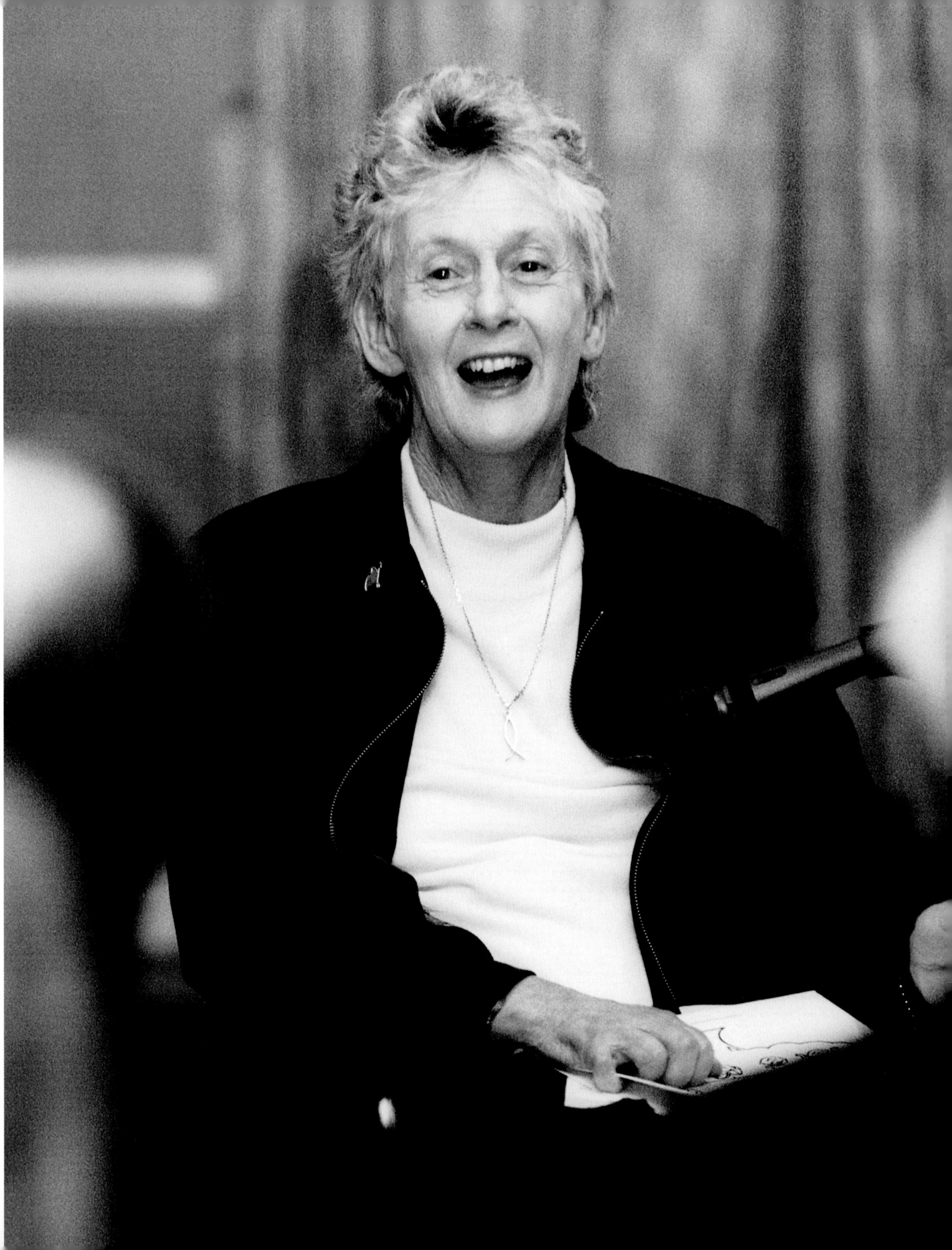

BETTY CUTHBERT PERSONAL COLLECTION

above: *Australia's first two Aboriginal gold medallists at the Olympics, Nova Peris (hockey) and Cathy Freeman (athletics), with Betty and Rhonda.*

opposite clockwise from top left: *two of Australia's 50 greatest Olympians, swimmer John Konrads and Betty Cuthbert; nine-time Olympic gold medallist Mark Spitz with Betty and Rhonda; Polish Olympic track and field legend, Irena Szewinska with Betty; multiple freestyle world-record holder Shane Gould with Betty; the Golden Girl receives a kiss from the future Governor of Victoria, John Landy.*

above (clockwise from top left): *admirers galore: Betty shares a laugh with long-time Queensland premier Joh Bjelke-Petersen; prime minister John Howard with the Golden Girl and Keith Gillam; talk-show host Michael Parkinson chats to Betty; swimmer Kieren Perkins with Rhonda and Betty.*

opposite (clockwise from top left): *Marjorie Jackson-Nelson, former prime minister Malcolm Fraser and Betty; the Golden Girl with Elton John; musician Peter Allen and Betty.*

above: *Betty's mother, Marion, was one of her greatest supporters. Marion and Betty at Government House, Sydney, where Betty was presented with the Order of Australia.*

left: *Proud mother and daughter: Here, Marion and a youthful Betty arrive at the Sydney Sports Ground for an afternoon of interclub competition.*

opposite: *Marion and Les plant kisses on their celebrity daughter during Tokyo celebrations in 1964.*

DAWN FRASER Betty and I have been friends since the 1956 Olympic Games and we've built up a friendship that has lasted ever since . . . I consider her one of my greatest friends.

Her legacy for sport in this country is that [her achievements] gave inspiration to a lot of young people to try and follow in her footsteps . . . As the Golden Girl in sport, that says a lot [about] the inspiration that she left—not only to young people as far as athletics is concerned, but also to young people for setting an example of how to behave in public.

It was a great shock to the system [to discover Betty had MS]. It was very upsetting. But knowing what type of battler she was, I knew that she would get through it . . . Even when she knew that she had MS, she still went on helping young people in their sport and that says a lot for her character.

My favourite memory of Betty Cuthbert is the fact that I saw her win that 100 metres event in Melbourne in 1956. I can still see her running down the track with her mouth wide open, and her flying through the air like she wasn't even touching the ground.

above: *Australia's three most successful female sprinters: Shirley Strickland, Marjorie Jackson and Betty Cuthbert.*

top left: *An extraordinary line-up: Raelene Boyle, Betty, Dawn Fraser and Marjorie Jackson.*

top right: *Dawn Fraser and Betty Cuthbert were the sprint champions of the pool and the track in Melbourne, and remain good friends.*

Betty committed herself 100% to her sport and captured the hearts of the Australian public. She has always shown amazing strength throughout her life.

MARJORIE JACKSON

Raelene Boyle and Murray Rose with Betty.

RAELENE BOYLE Bet was coaching when I first started to hit the scene where I was noted. I was very young for an athlete; I was selected for Mexico at the age of 16. Four years before that, I was only 12 when Betty ran at her last Olympics. So I didn't really know what it was all about when she was running . . . I was running for a club but didn't really know much about Betty Cuthbert or the Olympic Games. I was too busy playing footy and cricket in the streets with my brothers to watch the Olympic Games on television, which came in on newsreel.

I got to know Bet through my athletic career and we became quite good friends. And of course, Betty worked for Adidas and Adidas would have loved to have had me in their gear. But I wouldn't wear it. She, at one stage, told me that one of her jobs had been assigned to get to know me and try and get me to convert in shoes. And I really appreciated the fact that she told me that. We had a nice polite friendship. I really respect Betty.

One of the greatest honours I've ever been given was to push the wheelchair with Bet in it into the stadium in Sydney at the opening of the Olympic Games. It was a difficult time for me because I had just been diagnosed six weeks before with ovarian cancer, and had surgery. So I wasn't too well. Catching up with Bet is always a joy. I can remember the sheer delight in her face when we walked into the stadium. She was looking across her shoulder up at me and she had tears running down her face, and those beautiful blue eyes glistening. She was absolutely and totally delighted with the experience. And so was I. I was overjoyed to be given the honour of pushing such a great athlete into the stadium.

I think Bet was one of the greatest track and field athletes that this country has produced, be it male or female. At 18, to go out and win those gold medals in Melbourne was a fantastic inspiration and I'm sure accelerated the growth of women's track and field in this country at that time.

She's an inspiration the way she keeps going when everyone thinks that time isn't on her side.

Close family and friends who represent many of the most important relationships in Betty's life: Marion Cuthbert, Dawn Fraser, Midge Cuthbert, Rhonda Gillam, Betty and June Ferguson.

FRANCES ANDRIJICH

statistics

Betty Cuthbert competed in three Olympic Games and won four gold medals. In two Commonwealth Games, she won one gold and two silver medals. She set 10 individual world records and was a member of four world record breaking relay teams. She also won four national titles and 10 state titles.

Her career, like the careers of many other athletes, had its ups and downs and included a retirement of 16 months in 1960–61.

Betty made a successful comeback to win her fourth Olympic gold medal.

At the end of 1964, when Betty retired, she ranked number one in the world in the 100 yards (10.5 seconds) and second in the 400 metres behind North Korea's Sin Kim Dan's new but unratified world record of 51.2 seconds. She had dropped to equal 19th in the 220 yards with 23.9 seconds.

Betty's international career lasted eight years (1956–1964). She broke a world record in five of those years and was world ranked either number one or two in each of those years except 1961 when she was retired. She raced and beat nearly all her major rivals throughout her career and she still ranks twentieth on Australia's all-time list for 400 metres.

Betty's personal bests would rank her number one in Australia for 200 and 400 metres this year (2006); if she had run her personal bests at the 2006 Melbourne Commonwealth Games she would have finished sixth in both 200 and 400 metres.

In the following statistics, times—which were measured manually with a stop watch—are given in seconds. Where electronically recorded times are available, they appear in brackets and are marked with *.

career statistics

YEAR	EVENT	PLACING, DISTANCE AND TIME
1956	Australian Championships	3rd, 100 yards heat, 11.0
		1st, 220 yards, 25.0 (1st in heat, 25.5)
	Olympic Games	1st, 100 metres, 11.5 (11.82*) (1st in heat, 11.4; 2nd in semi, 12.0)
		1st, 200 metres, 23.4 (23.55*) (1st in heat 23.5; 1st in semi, 23.6)
		1st, 4x100 metres, 44.5 (44.65*) (1st in heat, 44.9, 45.00*)
	World Records	200 metres, 23.2, Sydney, 16 September
		4x100 metres, 44.9, Melbourne, 1 December
		4x100 metres, 44.5, Melbourne, 1 December
		4x110 yards, 45.6, Sydney, 5 December
		4x220 yards, 1.36.3, Sydney, 5 December
1957	NSW Championships	1st, 220 yards, 23.9
1958	NSW Championships	1st, 100 yards, 10.4
		1st, 220 yards, 23.5
	Australian Championships	2nd, 100 yards, 10.4 (1st in heat, 10.5)
		2nd, 220 yards, 23.5 (1st in heat, 24.6)
		1st, 4x110 yards, 46.0
	Commonwealth Games	4th, 100 yards, 10.7 (10.84*), (1st in heat, 10.8; 2nd in semi, 10.9)
		2nd, 220 yards, 23.8 (23.77*), (1st in heat, 24.5; 1st in semi, 24.0)
		2nd, 4x110 yards, 46.1 (46.12*), (1st in heat, 46.6, 46.71*)
	World Records	100 yards, 10.4, Sydney, 1 March
		220 yards, 23.6, Perth, 18 January
		220 yards, 23.5, Sydney, 8 March
1959	NSW Championships	1st, 100 yards, 10.6
		1st, 220 yards, 24.0
	Trans Tasman Cup	1st, 440 yards, 54.3
	World Records	440 yards, 55.6, Sydney, 17 January
		440 yards, 54.3, Sydney, 21 March

YEAR	EVENT	PLACING, DISTANCE AND TIME
1960	NSW Championships	1st, 100 yards, 10.4 (1st in heat, 10.2)
		1st, 220 yards, 23.9
	Australian Championships	2nd, 100 yards, 10.9 (1st in heat, 10.9)
		1st, 220 yards, 23.2 (1st in heat, 24.1)
		2nd, 4x110 yards, 46.6
	Olympic Games	4th in quarter final, 100 metres, 12.0 (12.18*) (2nd in heat, 12.1)
	World Records	60 metres, 7.2, Sydney, 27 February
		220 yards, 23.2, Hobart, 7 March
1961	Retired from competition	
1962	Commonwealth Games	5th in semi, 100 yards, 11.0 (11.13*) (2nd in heat, 11.1)
		5th, 220 yards, 24.6 (24.80*) (2nd in heat, 24.9; 2nd in semi, 24.3)
		1st, 4x110 yards, 46.6
1963	NSW Championships	1st, 100 yards, 10.9
		1st, 220 yards, 24.0
		1st, 440 yards, 54.7
	Australian Championships	3rd, 100 yards, 10.9 (1st in heat, 10.8)
		2nd, 220 yards, 23.7 (1st in heat, 27.8)
		1st, 440 yards, 53.3 (2nd in heat, 57.8)
		2nd, 4x110 yards, 47.1
	World Records	440 yards, 53.5, Melbourne, 11 March
		440 yards, 53.3, Brisbane, 23 March
1964	NSW Championships	3rd, 100 yards, 11.0
		2nd, 220 yards, 24.3
	Australian Championships	4th in heat, 220 yards, 25.9
		2nd, 440 yards, 54.3 (2nd in heat, 56.8)
	Olympic Games	1st, 400 metres, 52.0 (52.01*) (3rd in heat, 56.0; 2nd in semi, 53.8)

yearly progression

YEAR	100 YARDS	100 METRES	220 YARDS/200 METRES	440 YARDS/400 METRES
1953	11.0 (=4th)/10.9w	25.1y		
1954	10.9 (5th)/10.8w			
1955	11.0 (=17th)	11.9 (=17th)	24.8y (=21st)	
1956	10.6 (3rd)	11.4 (=1st)/11.2w	23.2 (1st)	
1957	10.6 (2nd)/10.4w		23.9y (=1st)	
1958	10.4 (=2nd)	11.8 (=23rd)	23.5y (2nd)	54.4 (2nd)
1959	10.5 (1st)	11.5w	23.5y (=1st)	54.3y (=2nd)
1960	10.4 (1st)/10.2w	11.5 (=5th)/11.3w	23.2y (2nd)	
1961	Did not compete			
1962	10.6 (=2nd)/10.6w		23.9w (=7th)	
1963	10.6 (=2nd)/10.6w	11.7 (=21st)	23.7y (8th)	53.2y (2nd)
1964	10.5 (=1st)	11.7 (=36th)/11.3w	23.9 (=19th)	52.0 (2nd)

World rankings are shown in brackets.

'w' indicates a wind-assisted time.

'y' indicates a 'yards' time.

For the yearly progression, manual times are shown.
Electronic timing was only used in Olympic and Commonwealth Games.
All world rankings were in manual times.